The sound of silence

By Anna Cellmer

First published in 2006 in Lulu Publisher

By Anna Cellmer

annaela3@gmail.com
http://stores.lulu.com/annaela3
https://www.facebook.com/pages/Daily-Crumbs-poetry-collections-by-Anna-Cellmer/152073201656457
https://www.facebook.com/opengatesbyAnnaCellmer
https://www.facebook.com/pages/Beautiful-Stranger-by-Anna-Cellmer/211403929016220
https://www.facebook.com/soundofsilencebyannacellmer
https://www.facebook.com/anna.cellmer
https://www.facebook.com/anna.cellmer.1

Copyright Anna Cellmer 2006

I dedicate this book to my first love
Thank you for stopping by in to my life even if just for a while

If not you I'll never know how much passion and freedom I have inside, thank you to be silent and patient through all this time.

01 – Insomnia
02 – Three nights in Zakopane
03 – The conqueror
04 – Mirror room
05 – The night's piety
06 – Underground
07 – Distance
08 – Calmness
09 – The Puzzle
10 – Wandering
11 – The kiss
12 – Meeting you once more
13 – Win the whiles
14 – Dance of love
15 – Waltz with death
16 – First night
17 – Far from you
18 – Dedication
19 – I'm Sarah
20 – Coming back to you
21 – Missing you
22 – To all special men I meet on my way
23 – Love prophecy
24 – Oh, my poor words!
25 – Waiting for you
26 – Lost lover
27 – Hidden in you
28 – Travelling thoughts
29 – The shadow
30 – Little days
31 – Secret
32 – Silence
33 – Melody
34 – Waves
35 – Just a piece of your heart
36 – Double life
37 – Beloved
38 – Visit
39 – Is it really too much?
40 – It is you
41 – Letters
42 – Are you waiting for me?
43 – You know you must love me
44 – Yes I want your love
45 – How could you leave me
46 – You are here for me
47 – What else can I show
48 – Don't be afraid
49 – No time to meet still
50 – Love letter fragment
51 – I'm just a woman in love
52 – I'm sorry my love
53 – Something happened
54 – Naked soul
55 – Queen of this game
56 – I'm here for you
57- There is nothing wrong in love
58- The show
59 – I just wish to know
60- So simple truth
61 – Regrets
62 – No, my love
63 – Thoughts
64 – Just come back to bed
65 – Can it just be a dream?

66 – Lesson
67 – Please don't be only a dream
68 – I can't believe
69 – Just come with me
70 – How come you!
71 – Is it our way to go
72 – You are mine, don't forget!
73 – I'm sorry my God
74 – Just a waste of the time
75 – Why is it so hard
76 – We are children of the earth
77 – I'm sorry, it's you who I miss
78 – I saw the news today
79 – I'm sorry for you terrorists
80 – Could you?
81 – When I'm in love with you
82 – I wish to be
83 – What is wrong with us?
84 – Destructive influence
85 – It's just a tool
86 – The illusion that you are here
87 – A drug
88 – Lost in forest
89 – Once we did love
90 – Please be for me
91 – How I wish to comeback to this place I can call heaven
92 – The differences
93 – I want you here
94 – Can you be this man?
95 – Hey where are you?
96 – We are free here
97 – The death of love
98 – Still waiting for the king
99 – What is this write actually
100 – I try to play
101 – I don't need your words at all
102 – A very simple dream
103 – I know it a lot of words I gave to you
104 – No, don't be friends
105 – A delicate case
106 – Dream
107 – I'm just a coward of love
108 – Don't be silent your whole life
109 – Can you forgive me now?
110 – I wasn't so strong
111 – How it's sad (be careful it's about sex)
112 – It's just a moment I need to realize that you are just a dream I have
113 – Let this dream come true
114 – Is it something wrong with me?
115 – Maybe this dream is all you need
116 – What are you going to do with me now?
117 – I shouldn't ask anything
118 – I'm so scared I let you feel not how I planned
119 – Do you read me?
120 – My life is so beautiful from the time I found you
121 – I wish to know your habits
122 – Do you know the cure for love?
123 – It's great to be on the same side
124 – Little fears
125 – Do you believe we could be together in real?
126 – How it's nice Mr. Blair
127 – Girl go to France for a little romance
128 – How to not lose this pleasure
129 – Internal fight
130 – How it'd be dark without all of us
131 – All you can do here

132 – Just yes or no
133 – All because of…
134 – I wish you here
135 – I don't see the reason why
136 – Yes or no I wish to know
137 – It's just I need to know if you wish the same, my love
138 – I'm ready for love
139 – I just hope you are happy with me
140 – Are you confused over me darling?
141 – Men be careful of young girls
142 – A thousand words
143 – Please don't be kind
144 – There is no point
145 – We have to finish this somehow
146 – Just stay where you are
147 – Invitation
148 – Could you touch me there?
149 – Don't be afraid to love me
150 – This moment when I knew
151 – What are you waiting for
152 – Pick up the phone please
153 – Sad advice
154 – Desert
155 – Mr. Traveller
156 – Cold inside
157 – Wicked game
158 – Yes I said goodbye
159 – I'm sorry that I'm happy
160 – Touch of love
161 – Every kind of love
162 – I wish to go to Paris with you
163 – Date on the boat
164 – I have to go
165 – No choice I have
166 – Hamburger
167 – Are you afraid I'm not serious?
168 – Life
169 – I know you are a good man
170 – Dear love
171 – Going to you
172 – This is the end
173 – Be realistic you said
174 – Can I come back?
175 – Just one thing
176 – Mix of emotions
177 – Just live a while
178 – You were as you should be
179 – The most I love to be in love
180 – Thank you to let me dream
181 – I loved you but
182 – You were cold enough
183 – Be a realist
184 – I didn't want anything wrong
185 – Happy dreamer
186 – Real life is never the same
187 – The sense of my life
188 – Do your thing
189 – About all these things that make us happy or sad
190 – I was just lost in my mind
191 – Who could suppose
192 – Little pleasures
193 – Just a drop
194 – Not everything depends on you
195 – No it wasn't so nice
196 – Never again
197 – You never know this

198 – Exciting experience
199 – I wouldn't be right to you
200 – Princess on the beach
201 – Princess has some troubles now
202 – Do I love you?
203 – There must be something wrong with me
204 – Just believe in something
205 – What do I want
206 – Meanings
207 – Meanings in life
208 – Another touch
209 – I like the way you look at me
210 – The time between
211 – You were not only one man of my life
212 – Some dream should stay like that
213 – This is the way
214 – You won't be there
215 – The pleasure of love
216 – Just a little sign of you
217 – Hard work - never
218 – I'm not in love anymore
219 – Just another touch
220 – Request to the broken hearted one
221 – I'm sorry but
222 – Do you know the value of you?
223 – You have enough time to not hurry up
224 – The art of life
225 – Come back, my lord
226 – Important things for today
227 – To my poet friend
228 – Dear God
229 – It's hard sometimes
230 – Simple needs
231 – Fellow passengers
232 – For you
233 – I owe to you, my love
234 – I know you never meant to break my heart
235 – Fed by dreams
236 – Hello my friend here
237 – Valentine
238 – Quite ironic
239 – How come you do this Anna
240 – The doors
241 – No need to see you
242 – Little sign

Insomnia

My hands wander about a thicket of delusions
They go for the rhythm of rocking remembrances
The threads weave joining it with moments of happiness
They rock to sleep its unfulfilled dreams
They build inexpressible divine unreality
They compress - desirous to hug all mankind,
Helpless they shove after the edges of bed
They perish in the darkness shameless, naked and thirsty
Until they are put to sleep lying on the sheet powerlessly.

They know more than I'm able to say
They still feel this what was so long ago
They are the memory of the past moments
They are the imagination of events which hasn't been
They are you and me and all that is
And what lacks, they live and feel
Though they are feed with only homesickness continually
They are as spirits which never experienced the quiet
They wander continually, helpless in the face of their own torment

Three nights in Zakopane

I ran to you on meeting
And I became drunk on your closeness
We plunged to each other
And we fell amazed
Lasting in this joyful intoxication
We couldn't find a place
In bed of our amusement
Laughing

I trembled as a leaf
In the gust which you were
With cold and fright
Before the storm which fell on me
I clung to you
How I would want to conceal myself in you
And you trembled yet more strongly
Apologizing...

You uncovered me
Now I had to find you
In darkness, blindfolded
You led me, you helped
Because alone I was yet too shy
In order to look before me
I felt guilty now
Sacrilege.

The conqueror

You entered on my territories
You mastered them without question
Like William the Conqueror
I kept silent, expressing agreement
With your English imperialism
And now what, you resign?
Then fear tells you to put out
This what you earlier lighted
You want peace suddenly
You play the diplomat
You want friendship but you forgot
But a moment ago
You already had almost all.

Mirror Room

Irreplaceable
You are reflected in everyone,
The sight, the palm,
the mouth
My Mirrored room
Everywhere you
And only you
Even in his eyes different
Even in his embraced
Tool of caress
Replaceable
Not good enough
To take your place
On the other side of the mirror
Soon I will find a stone

To break all this glass around!

Out naivety!
Out illusion!

It is me who is left
And my emptiness
I don't want anything
Your circulating husbands
Your handles and tongues
Asking about so little
And you as well
All you are nothing but escape

I can't break anything
Because you are my reflection
All and you this exceptional one too
Without you I am like a mirror
In a room without light
In a darkness
I don't see anything there is no me
So I go out on meeting you
To see myself again
In my reflection
To not forget that I exist.

The night's piety

I entered to the dark corridor
Of two bodies
Intertwined with a hope
Of the common morning
To vanish
In this sweet incapacity
The world of the night's piety
And you wandered
With the fear to find
Uunsuitable gates
For which you could
Discover too much
You penetrated shyly
Aimlessly – into the dream

Underground

I go down underground
The hazard of existence
And I am in this tunnel
Of delightful submission
Windingly
With the laughter
I bite through fetters
Of reasonable honesty
And I drown in the puddle
Of ecstatic repugnance
Insecure tomorrow

Distance

I don't feel you so strongly now
Your smell grows flat
It stayed only
An empty gust of oblivion
Your eyes walk away
How birds flock
Disappearing in the blue of the ocean
But I stay here
Pressing in my small world
Again putting to shame
My own steps
And hands without support
I am not already strong
Loneliness wraps around me its overcoat
We become one
It is my soul
I became its incarnation
I got lost in it
I do not know where I am
I don't know who I am
It is everywhere.

Calmness

The priestess of calm normality
Lives here temporarily
She tries to cover the skies
Black chaos of the nonentities
She smiles condescendingly
Reconciled with the world
I measure her time
When she will fall out from the corner
When she will meet with an accident
And I will jump in the precipice again.

The puzzle

Closed in the tin of my own
I forgot about the essence of the world
Remembered in this dance
Whirling, I come in more and more deeply
Inwards of my own images
But it's not me who is the riddle
On which all look for the answer
Nor even none of you
We are only the element of the puzzle
In order to find
A right place in suitable time
In order to not destroy the world
In order to not overlook its chance
Of participation in evolution of the life
And then look into the eyes
With pride - not shame...

Wandering

I've got lost in this way to you
constantly wandering aimlessly
looking for beauty in space
but what is it for?
When I still go to you
And seeing you I go away
Because it is still too far
Even standing face to face
Distance doesn't get smaller
So I run away further
To a feeling that I lose again
Crying to miss you again
No ocean will cover me your eyes
No mountain routes will make me forget...
And however I err further
having a hope that once
I won't need to go away

The kiss

I run through the rainbow
Drenching my mouth
In the pastels - tints
Of its passing,
Absorbing every touch of its colour
This warmth I love,
It pulsates in blood,
And I penetrate
Across its variety,
Pages of you
To become only
The small particle
Drinking from your mouth
My own soul

Meeting you once more

You returned in dreams again
About the blue of your eyes
So sweet…
About kisses
So delightful
And about touch
So penetrating,
So true…
How every word
Sunk in memory
Of our moments
You've feed me
The sight of you
And you are in me again
How alter ego
How the answer
For all the questions
How reassuring
For uncertainty
How the source of new hope
Not ending
The history of our hearts.

Win the whiles

I shifted the figures
Running into you
Pawns in this game of life
We move with grace
On the chart of existence
Coming across
On the king, the proper movement
The Victory
A while of authenticity
In this game of feelings
Then there is the smile of the sun
On chosen faces
Maybe fleeting
But it's worth
Every time
To win the whiles

Dance of love

Every little step runs out in the future
Which iss nothing but a moment
We live for
So I make sure myself
That you are, that you wait
There for this time
When again you will cover my world
And I will see only
The smile of your eyes
So sweet
I wait for the darkness
From which you will go out
To take me
Inwards of your soul
I wait for the palms
That kidnap me for the fire
In which we will burn
When again it absorbs us
This dance of our hearts

Waltz with death

I touch the interior of a black abyss
And I feel death in my hand
I turn her over in my fingers
I dance with her in the moonshine
The shameless waltz of my dark thoughts
I penetrate her incorporeality
And I feel that I have her in me
She is the miraculous well
In which I would like to sink every day
And touch her soul,
And tear to pieces her heart
To absorb all
What is concealed before me.

First night

I gave myself up today
For you
Near you
Though it was not you near me,
I gave myself up
Giving nothing more
Except me
And you do not even know
How this a little.

I cried today
By you
Near you
Though you didn't
See my tears
I cried
Feeling nothing more
Except sorrow
That this is not you
Who lies by me.

Far from you

The trip the next day
An unnecessary trip
Which I dedicate to you
How every action
Even this the most prosaic
I look at the world
In order to know more
In order to give you
Still more
I fear only
To lose you en route
I fear
That I will not find the road
To you
Because I will go too far
Because I will crash
Skipping in to the precipice
From which there
Is no return.

Dedication

I'm with you
For your hands giving me delight
For life that you feed me
For memories still alive
For music, for wine
For this trip into the unknown
For you I'm
For the loneliness that I kill
For the moment of happiness that I give
For laugh that I infect
For the adventure that you wanted

I'm Sarah

I am Sarah, drowsy and wet
To worship his deity
On different ways
I am woman trippant
World right next to
Leaving remembrance
I am a cloud which the wind
Propels over the ground
I am a shadow which you touch
And I disappear
Because I do not exist for you

Coming back to you

I forgot
For a moment
About your existence
Immersed in a dream
In reality
Gorged with delicacies
of the World
Passed me on tray
With a wine binding
I walked away
To stop for a moment
Think about you
And I come back now
Yours again
Washed from sin
By love
To you
Even without you
Even not with you
Always yours.

Missing you

I still look for you
I miss you all the time
Listening with attention in the silence
One's small sadness
And sweet joys
I'm a reflection
The events of a day and night
To stand up again
Before the wall
of Silent loneliness
Closed somewhere
There, in the centre
Of my being
Deaf to words
An insecure nobody
Wanting nothing
Abstract from the world
Perfect and beautiful
In one's hopes
On self annihilation.

To all special men I meet on my way

I like you
These who I meet
On my way
I like these halts
A silent agreement
I like your eyes
Full of understanding
So similar and speaking
More than your mouth
Though they also speak
This truth so well known
Because my own
Sometimes undiscovered
But more significant
I like you
Less than Lovers more than friends
Who knows more from others
Those who never had any chance
To perceive this path
Which is possible to pass together
Even if only
To the first crossing road

Love's prophecy

Sunken by you
Forever
I became a shell
Listening with attention, waiting,
For the high tide
You would tackle me
Inside you
Relishing
The magnitude of your love
My ocean
The most ubiquitous

Every road
That takes me away
From you
Is incorrect
Every moment
Even the merriest
Far from you
Is lost
Because only you are
My source of love
And my happiness
The most essential
So I wait
Turning back
From the incorrect roads
Which I tread
Wanting a moment
To get away
From your power
In vain
When the moon also
Prompts me the words
That I'm yours
How could I
Not believe it?
When even my heart
Laughs
Into the sweetest
Prophecy
How could I
Distrust my heart
Which screams
For you, and it knows
That it is you!

Oh, my poor words!

Imprisoned in the category of the one small picture
I became the slave of affectionate sentimentality
Asking myself about the magnitude
In name of words - the pretenders of Love
O, mad words
Desirous more than you can receive,
Do not ask about the fame
And the name of the Poetry
Of the Ages Size
Because you've been sewn

Nothing but one person measure
Looking of the second one

The small picture of lyrical magnificence
Choke further
In your longing town
Because it isn't time yet
For creation of the new dimensions

You are too young still
To such terrific transubstantiations
You are as The Little Prince
Who could stir up too much
In this world of undiscovered values
By his defiant orders
So paint yourself further
The crystal small picture
Until you will grow up to the perfection
And you will shoot
Of the thousand crystalline flowers
Which become rooted in the ground
That the sons and daughters would be born

The Masters and Margaritas
Gods and constructors
The new order of the world.

The sparkling herds
The imps of Idleness
Pierce me thoroughly
That they would extricate oneself
The pearly Mass
Of Impertinent Blaze
The uncontrollable Joy

O, my poor words!
You felt ashamed because you don't know
Whether you have something to say – to this world
You got scared

This tale about yourself
But this it is not a crime
You can play with yourself
To arrange in the sky constellations
To get to the core of essence of the matter
And to die, uncovering nothing new

You can play in the gravediggers
Or the scatterers more
Nobody keeps you under command
Because it is me who keeps the reins
Of this Carriage of Words
And I love this rough ride and laugh
Of my own words
Speeding up to the unconsciousness
How the fiery Arabs
On the new road
To obscene and disobedient
Unknowing

So drive further!
My pearly steeds
To the unknown distinction
To the open sensuality
To the beginning of endlessly
Or with the many ends

To a peak of iceberg
Inside of impenetrable nothingness
Wherever
You can take me
Where I will die
Whipped and whipping
The Whip of contempt and the revolt
Against Everything
What dares my attention
That I'm going too fast
Or maybe in the wrong direction.
Oh, fool unbelievers
Of Existence the open border with the miracle!

How come you arrest me on the road
How come you don't believe in my Words?
Rushed on the cards
To the Meeting of the Perfect Truth?
I laugh to you with the words

Which are playing with themselves
Stimulating my soul
To the Orgasm of Survival
And what else I can expect
From these words which don't care about the fame?

Waiting for you

I swung with branches
A tree without roots
Free in space
Summoning it to flight
With every day
Its crown grows
Liberated by the pressure
Of the corset of youth
They would rustle so
So loudly
Summoning its lover
Who it lives for
Who it dances for
The wild dance of nature
Among the rocky hills
Together with the wind
Playing on the waves
Melody bursts of passion
I call You
My lover
Among the night
I call You
The hum of the wind
I call You
The scream of the storm
You would crash
There on the island
Where I wait
If you want
I will be a willow
To be able to
Wreathe Your shoulders
So that You could hear
The melody of the bird's wings
Fluttering among the branches

If you want
I will be a rock
Where You will reach
Looking for refuge
After a long cruise
If I could
To take You in
Exposing all the caves
In which you could fall asleep
You could be a discoverer
You could wander
Over pulsating valleys and hills
You could conquer all the hilltops
You could find the roads to fiery cave
And I will feel Your every movement
You will touch me
With the sounds of music
Which you will feel in your heart
You will be the pianist
Which will play on me
The song awakening to the life
I call to You
My Dear
Standing on the rocks,
Gazing at the Ocean
Dressed in a gown
Of gossamer and fog
And with a necklace of morning dew
You would arrive to marry me
Because I'm Your goddess
Sailor
I call hopeful
That you will land on the island
Where I wait.

Lost lover

You got lost my dream lover
Your ship sank
In the depths of life
Among which you forgot
Where you have to swim
You crashed on the rocks
Which I poured out
From the last tears I shed for you
I am free now
In the isolation of this place
Expectant of betrothed
I go there now where he waits
This one who is and will be
And to whom I'm whispering
And he is so close
That I hear his voice
Even when he keeps silent,
The one who I feel
The one who I see
The one who is me
Because I am his

Hidden in you

Hiding myself
Under the cover
Of mine and your feelings
I don't remember anymore
This clearing
That I was running through
Some time ago
Still looking there for you
And now I'm living here
In our little world
So full of us
Where there is no place
For others
Or even for the wings
They could cover the picture
You and me
You for me
Me for you
I put off my wings
To not fly away
To feel your warm
Every day and night beside
I fill my space by you.

Travelling thoughts

November nights of great cities
Where the hotel- love dies
Torn with the anchor of life
With the scream spitting out the world
Again, with the future
I rummage the time in rubbish heaps
To find the essence of the rights
Ruling over immortality

Dipped in the twilight of space
Swing with hips to raise the laughter
Which overfills me through and through
To shout no existing names
To express a charm tells
Which are thundering sluggishly
Through the waves
Caressing my soul
By unremembered songs of the world.

The gentle space raises my body
To pour on himself with the surface
Seeking of the liberation
Somewhere behind the horizon
Of the Uncertainty
The Life depends of the power of shoulders
Groping for
the Resting-place
Would be possible to come back home
And at this time?

The shadow

I find myself in the shadow
As a stranger
Who takes a part in this life
By accident
Almost as an intruder
Who doesn't know the rules
Of this game
I try to put on a brave face
This that within me I do not really care
Of the things so close to me
The deepest love we feel
Is this far away
This that we can't touch
Looking far on the horizon
That we reach on the stars
But not this one which is so close
To become everyday life
So simple as the baby's cry
Demanding to change its nappy
But I'm coming back to you
Seeing you covering boys
While you look at them
With such tenderness
That tears put away
This internal voice
Which is pushing me
To the circle of magical dreams
That are stifling
This love with the smell of life

Little days

I live the natural rhythm of everyday life
To step by days in a year
The saint deliberation without
Anger for all these little events around
Which are creating my reality right now
Without inspiration of not realizing teenager anymore
The wild chariots of passion
Are gone
And I'm mixed with some comical
Little things
I take this rule seriously
That is imposed to me by life
Not sure of aims
I should go for
Not sure of methods
I use every day
Sure only you
That you forgive me
Every uncertainty I have within.

After years….

Secret

I gushed
Betraying my secret
Stored already
In the secret chest
Of my being
God's whether you know
How does happiness look?
Because I know
I am happiness
My heart sings
The sun lit me
Again
I love, I love,
I love!
And only this matters
And you know this.

Silence

You keep silent
You don't know again
What to do
With this love
It crushed you
So suddenly
That you gnaw on your thoughts
What to answer
On such a call
And now
Maybe you've already forgot
Where this way leads
Where you never went
Lover
My cold English Man
Don't be so cold for me
Just let me love you
Or let me go
Because you are my desire
Until I will be sure
That you are dead to me
I just need to know
What your heart
Is telling you
About me.

Melody

No one feels this same melody
In his heart
As I do
Even you
All you are
Just an imagination
No one can
Feel this same
Orient express with dance
As I do
No one can
Give me
This orgasm
That I need
Even you can't
I'm alone again
At this simple world
With its roles
Without any sense
Just simple giving
And simple taking
Little, little things to do
To make each other comfortable
I can't stand that situation
I want here
The life comes true
My Truth
With all meanings
In your tongue
In your lips
In your hands and voice
And the music
In my heart.

Waves

I touched the sky yesterday
Feeling you again
So strongly merrily
And today?
I fell suddenly
Because I didn't know
What to say
That would understand me
One your smile
Happiness
Moment of hesitation
And this " OK I will call you later "
Charm splashed
I am on the bottom
I turn back
I run away
I dismiss all
What to do?
When you are so close
But it hurts so strongly
You gave me happiness
But I don't know
Will I survive
This time
Trying again
Calling to your heart

Just a piece of your heart

No one knows me better now
Than you
And you know
What you can't do
You are just wonderful
I'm ready for anything
That is why
You can't be mine
It is too late
For us, my Love
You are strong
And you are good
You are everything
That I have inside
I was hiding you for so long
And now you know
That you must stay
In my dream's zone
Forever... but...
How I'd like again to
Have just piece of your heart
In my hand

Double life

Double life
Two marriages
On real
And with you
Always yours
In my heart
Double voices
About me and you
That all I feel is true
That you are my life
And it is not only a dream
That you are mine
All the time
here

And the second one
Voice about the things
What just have gone
With these few days
And you can't believe
That it is love
Because you were on time
To go away
From me

Beloved

What can I do my Beloved
That I'm happy enough
Only when I love you
Only when I see you
As a man I dream about
As my wonderful knight
I'd like to thank you
For your beauty
For your face so sweet to me
For your voice so tender
For the eyes I remember
Were always so joyful to me
I want to dream about you always
My Lover from old days
I'll never forget you my Love
Your picture is always above
Every day and every night
I feel your understanding sight
And this is so much to me
That it just used to be
Forever.

Visit

Are you single?
I am asking because...
I'd like to visit you
Someday
Some night
I'd like you to wait
For me
Alone
That's why I ask
I just need to come
To you
But I don't know
Your address
Is it a problem for you
That I'm going
To visit you
Without my clothes?

Is it really too much?

Is it really too much for you?
This one night what I'm asking for?
It doesn't matter what we will do
Making love or not to
I just want to lie in your arms again
To feel your smell and hear your breath
I'd like to kiss your mouth
Is it too much for you?
Please give me just this
I can wait as long you wish
But promise me
That you will be waiting
For me
But for now you can stay there
I need to feel you in the air.

It is you

I don't know
How it happened
That I'm yours again
I'm standing
Between you
And the world I have
To see
That only you
Are real to me

Even missing you
All my life through
Is better than
Everything I have
Because
It's you
Who makes me feel
So good

Letters

Sending letters
Is it a good idea
For love?
But how
Can I have you
Now
If I was so stupid
To go away
So many times
before
To forget
Who I belong to
My heart is with you
Is it honest
To be with you
Like this
And live
Without you?
But I don't care
I must do it
There is no way
My heart can't stop this fight

Are you waiting for me?

I hope you are waiting for me
Because I'll come to you
Sooner or later but I'll do it
There is no other way to me
Maybe you are waiting
For my doctorate to be finished?
Maybe you are waiting for
My children to grow up?
Maybe you are waiting
For me to come to you
Without any letter anymore?
I don't know
But I'll do it
You know
So, you are silent
You don't have to speak
Because you know
That I belong to you
Don't you?

You know you must love me

You know
You must love me
Or break my heart
Because your silence
Is too ambiguous
Too exciting for me
And this way
You make me
Your slave
Forever
Don't you see this?
Do you want this?
Really?
Oh, how long
You will tease me
This way
I didn't know
That you are
So cruel a man
And you will play
With me
At this silent game
But just don't be scared
To speak with me
Just don't hide
Behind me
That you love me
I'll be calm I promise
I'll wait when the time
Will come
For us
Just don't forget
To tell me
What do you really feel
All right?
I wont resign
From you, my Love
Not this time
When I'm so sure
When I know
That you are
My only Love
I have inside
My soul

Yes I want your love

Yes I don't want
Just to sleep with you
I want your love
I want to read your soul
But you
You are afraid to show me
Yourself again
Why?
What is wrong, my Love?
If you love me
I'm yours
If you don't
I'll understand
So don't worry
Please
Just open your heart
To me
I love you
I beg you
Just be my friend
If there is nothing else I can gain.

How could you leave me

How could you
Leave me
Without your hands
On me
Without your lips
In such a cold place
As Poland is
Do you think it was easy
To live
So many Years
Without your kiss?
How could you do this
To me, my Love
To your lady
To your miss
To your sweetie pie
And your piece?
Do you see
How it looks now?
When I still miss you
But you know
I'm somebody else
Wife right now
And you know
That this is maybe wrong
That I feel
What ten years ago
But what to do
If I'm still in love?
So please just wait
Awhile
Because I know what to do
To be with you.

You are here for me

Do you doubt yet
Why you are in my land?
Don't you understand
Your role in my life?
I need you, my Love
As a lover from my dreams
Can you be this man I mean?
Please show me
How wonderful you are
How deep love you can give
Please start to be with me
For real
I want you
Come to me
My Lover
This is all
What I'm living for
For love like this
Without any borders
Without any rules
Just come to me
At nights
Please
I didn't know
That loving you
And telling you about this
Can bring me so much joy
Yes, love to you
It's what I'm living for
But it's not sad love anymore
I'm so free
I can tell you everything
You don't have any idea
How it's a wonderful feeling
To have you inside my being

What else I can show

It's almost a year
When you came back
To my heart again
And I feel so well
With you inside
But Darling
I don't know
Your side
And what else
I can show you
That you could believe
That I love you
I said all I had to say
To make you feel the way
I feel too
Now it's time
To meet
Because I lack the arguments
I think I used them all
What else I can do for you
To make you sure
That you are only one man
I love

Please just let me come
And you will know
Everything about my soul
From my eyes, lips and hands
I will show you again
How love looks in reality
That you could understand
All my words
I wrote to you
Here.

Don't be afraid

I just don't understand
Why you can't speak with me
My friend
Is it because I was too strong?
I was too open for you?
Telling you what I want?
Do you find me too hot
Or sometimes too sad?
But don't be afraid
I don't have any altar
With your picture
To pray
You are the Love of my life
I have you inside
And I needed to tell you
About this
But now I feel free
I can do
What will be
The best
For you and me
So don't worry
And try to think
How to keep the touch
With me
Because I'm waiting
And I always will be
Your girl
In my dreams.

No time to meet still

If you are not ready
To answer my phone
It means to me
That you are not ready
To meet me
So maybe we shall wait
For better time
For us
But really
I still don't know
What your silence means
This: "No comment"
Or "Come to me"
It is the mystery still
And I can think
About this other few years
If you wish but please
Just don't blame yourself
About anything
Because I know I was too young
For you yet
And you needed to go
To find your own world
But it's you
Who is the ray
Of my sun, of my hope
In the deep of my heart
I never went
With another man so far
And that's why I try so much
To find a way to keep the touch
But I'm afraid that
It wasn't a good idea to write
And maybe this way
I just lost you again.

Love letter fragment

Love must be just a while
In reality
And eternity
In your mind after
I know this
I feel this
I experienced this
You are the proof
Of my new theory
Yes, you my Love
So much years far away
This quickly light
In my life
For real
But don't worry
This light stayed
Inside me
Besides I found you
I can speak again
It's wonderful
Don't you think?

Please lose your head
It will be so nice
If you could do it to me
You wont regret
I promise
You are a little bit
Too strong
With this silence
So long, I think

Come on, come talk to me
You are worth so much to me
You don't need to be so hard
Let's think how to tell me
About your wishes now

Yes you didn't come
To meet me some time ago
But you called
And now
It's all I have
To build my dream
To be brave
And to write, Having hope

That you want this

You don't know
How it's sometimes difficult
To believe
That all I do
Is nice for you
Because you love me

Yes because
I know how it is
If you are not in love
And someone try
To be so nice
And you know
That he just waste the time
Because you are cold

But you were never cold to me
You've just been silent too long
Am I wrong?
But I must give you some advice
Don't try to pretend
Just tell me
What I meant for you
I really need to know
I'm waiting so long
Please do it for me
And tell me or show
What do you feel
Because it's not easy for me
To live with my family
When I see you
So strong, so intensively
I'm still waiting for you
I don't know what to do
To change this

It's your turn, my Love
To be honest, to be sure
Let me come to you
And please don't treat me
As an idiot
Only because
I still love you
And I'm writing
Poems about this
It's just once

I'm like that in my life
And only to you
You should be happy
I'm rather reasonable girl
Mostly
No one knows me as a woman
So crazy for the man
I'm sorry if it's too much for you
To stand
I didn't know
I'll do it for you
But I have to

Collecting a whiles
It's not bad idea
They are not heavy
So you can bring them
Everywhere you go

These are moments when I agree
With that situation
That you are silent
And maybe it's better
Perhaps it's the best way
To be with you
Right now like that
Maybe if we meet
If we would try to be together
It wont work at all?
It will be too difficult?
I don't know
But most of the time
I think that I'd like to try.

If you want
We don't need to talk
About the past
Just tell me
Is it nice to you
What I'm doing now?
Is it nice for you
That I love you?

I don't have a choice
I see you all the time
You don't know

How it's difficult to stop
I just can't concentrate
Seeing you in my bed
Even making love to him
Especially then
I can't stop to talk to you
So I don't have the choice
I'm in love,

I just can
Stop to write to you
If you wish
But it wont change
This what I feel
So maybe it's better
To tell you
It's better if you know
That you are still here
And you can't remove
And that I don't know
What to do
To be with you
And that this is all
I wish
But the worst is
That he is so good
I shouldn't hurt him
And I don't know
How to do it
If I want to be with you
And the children yet
Could they feel all right
Could they understand
The new situation?
In a new apartment
With you as a my partner?
It could be difficult
But maybe just
At the beginning?
Maybe after some time
It will be all right?
And my husband
Could visit us
And take them
To him for some time?
And we all could be friends?
I don't know
Is it possible

But it works
With his first son
That's why
I can believe
That it could be
Possible but
What do you think
About this?

I can't explain
Why I'm like that
Why I think about
Destruction of my family
But
I see you all the time
I can't stop
I know it's mad
Loving you
After so many years
Just because
I found you again
And I heard your voice
And It was
So sweet to me
And I was so happy
But what do you feel?
My Love
How do you find
Your role in my life
Now
So special

Do you love
To be loved by me?
Do you love, me?

I didn't know
That this year
I'll start to live
So intensively
In my secret life
But you are
Again inside and
What can I do
For that
You are so wonderful to me?
That I can't find
Another topic

So interesting
To live
Love is all I need
And you are my love
From the first day
I saw you
And still
I just don't understand
Why we are not together
I know I talk too much
About my love to you
But I can't find
Other words
To speak with you
I'm sorry
I'm so mono-topic
I hope you don't find
It's boring

For me it's just
A sense of my existence
It's all I believe
I'm sorry I'm so simple girl
Do you think
We should speak
Rather about the politic?
All right
I can tell you
That your Blair is a quite nice man
What else
I'm really sorry
Because of the war
But maybe
It wasn't so bad
To try to win with
Osama Ben Laden?
And Hussein?
They are not a good men
But war is never great
So many people died
Again no sense with that
People fight
Oh let's not talk about this so much
It's hard sometimes to understand some of the men
Who are there on the top and who speaks in our name
So, maybe let's talk about your land?

British culture

what do I mean?
It's John Lennon
The Rolling Stones
I know you
From the history
About the conquerors
Henry XVIII
Queen Elisabeth too
And Irish conflict through
You have a nice queen
You have a Hyde Park
In London
You are rather friends of us
Excluding the Yalta Pact
You have a nice
A Prime Minister now
You are known
In this World
But this what I remember the most
Is one Englishman
In Jersey born
And all I believe is
That love is all I need
This simple truth
In all culture
From the Lennon's lips
What I also believe
But love is not so
Simple now, I know
But all I can say
Is that I just can't
Forget
And I can't
Just let you go again.

I think there in one big danger
That all love I have for you
I'll give you in these letters
And then
I'll stop to need to meet you in reality
So if you don't want this
I think that you should think
About the date of our meeting
This or next Year, ok?
Yes maybe this is not the best moment
To be together
But if only for one night?
Could it be all right?

I'm just a woman in love

I didn't know that I will share
The fate of all these
Women in love
Who care about the man's touch
Sending him too much
Messages, and letters
But I haven't found yet
A better way
To show you how I care
And as you know
I'm terribly scared
That it was the wrong way
And now
You will never want
To speak with me to come
Because maybe
You are afraid of this love
Or perhaps
You just don't want
To destroy this
Life I've built so far
which I can't see right now
Because it's only you
Who exists In my world
But you know
When you have children
It's not so simple
To change the place
Or the man you live with
If you have inside
Just a rest of responsibilities.

I'm sorry my love

I'm sorry my love
But I don't have
Much more force to get you
Maybe you are right
It's rather man's job
I give up I don't want
Anything anymore
Just don't forget that I love you
Just don't be scared
To come someday
When you will want this , OK?
Just remember
That my doors are always open for you
And that I miss you
In the deep of my heart I'm keeping you
And I'll always have you some way
And maybe someday
We will share our lives In reality
And thank you again
That you left me with this hope

Naked soul

What do you feel
Looking at my naked soul?
So clear
So open for you my dear?
Sitting alone at home
I think
How to capture
My love
In words
To take you
Inside my thoughts
I love to live
At this world
Full of you
My lord

Something happened

Something happened
Ten years ago
I met my love
And suddenly
Time stopped
I was reborn
I was so happy
To know that I love
Even when you've been gone
Even staying alone at home
Because I believed in your words
And I knew that
You just need some time
To fix your things around
And you will be coming back
To be my man as when it started
So I waited for you
So happy and so sad too
Because it wasn't simple
To love you without you
When you were always
So far away from this place
When you were so silent
But after some time
When I started to live
In the world of different feelings
I became shy and scared
That you are not real
So you turn into
My lover from dreams
But now, against everything
When you are so close again
I'm more strong to believe
That I can be for you
This one girl you need

Queen of this game

I change my name
Almost every day
Once I start to be brave
And I see myself
So strong, so great
As a queen of this game
As a woman from your dream
As the Athena with
The sword of words
To win this premier price
You, I mean
But you know
That sometimes I'm so weak
And I can't even speak
Standing so close to you
And I don't know at all
What to do with this heart
So broken-down, so afraid of
This real truth or of even you
And this life too
Please help me
To understand
What should I do
To be with you
My friend.

I'm here for you

My sweet man
I'd like to ask you
For something today
I'd like to know if you could love me this way
I'd like to know if you could read and enjoy what I say
Just like this
I'd like to be your private distraction
I'd like to be your favorite poet too
I'm here for you
That you would live within this dream land
Just with me
I realized that I have already found
The place for me and you in this world,
So, you know that you have my heart
But how do you feel with that?

I'm here to describe my dreams
To open your eyes for these secrets of art
That are natant from my heart
That are taken from your charm
My open soul is carrying you to this world
Where you should exist, my love

I'm this woman who lives in your dreams
So watch me and try to play fair
Within this game called love,
By the way, this play is for you
That you could know me well
With all the best I can give
To the man

I'm happy with you like this
I can dream about you always
But I need this dream to live
Do you think we could be
Together like this in reality?
And at last baby, don't forget
You let me to do this again
You let me drown in you
Because you didn't say "no"
When I was asking you
To stop me on this way to you
If you don't feel you could take this
And now is too late, my sweet
I just would like to believe that some day
You could tell me what do you think

About all these feelings I share with you
And with the whole world too.
There is nothing wrong in love
There is nothing wrong in love

Do you think
I shouldn't love you still
After so much time
We haven't seen each other?
Do you think
That I just lost my mind?
Or maybe it's just imaginary?
Do you find me unreal or funny?
Please check me, my love
Don't wait too long
I know it looks strange
I know it doesn't make sense
All these feelings I have but
Why I cry, when I think that
I should maybe give up
Because I already have
The family
Because you are still
So far away from me
Because you are silent again
But I can't, I can't forget
And how come you come back
To this land where I am
You are so free and so strong and so alone
Don't you understand it hurts me?
I almost feel your breath
I see your face and I just can't
I can't forget
I feel as a loser now only because
I wasn't strong enough to wait for you
I dreamed about you a few Years
The next few I tried to forget
And when you are back why I'm married?
But you are so afraid to meet me
Why it's so hard to tell me
What do you feel with that?
I don't want to pay for my mistake like this
I don't agree so I must be strong
To believe, my love
When nothing is told
I can change everything
Because nothing is wrong
In love.

The show

The show part one
I'm here only one
But I'm glad
If I can touch your heart
And I hope you feel well
With me inside this game
Called life, by the way
Looking at my side
Of this dream
This fairy land
Where we can be
As one, you and me
Inside this mystery
Where I can play
This role for you only
But what the end
You find the best, my love?
You are inside
This play, you know
Even as a silent man
You are taking a part
At this scene.

I just wish to know

All I want from you now
Is just that you could tell me
What do you feel
I'd like to know
Do you love me or not
It is just a few words
Then I'll be sure
That I'm here for you
And I'm not alone in this world
I don't need anything more
Just this word
I know how to live
Without you baby
But I want to believe
In this dream
Where you let me be within
So just make me sure
That I'm yours
Just this
I really don't expect more
I just wish to know.

So simple truth

My sweet boy, my love
Today I believe
So strong
That you love me too
And I feel so good
It is so simple truth
When I believe in this
I'm happy
When I try to give up
I don't feel good with that
So I'm in love
Oh, my boy
How I'd like to hold your hand again
Before it was all my fault
I was running away
All the time, all these years
But now I turn around
I'm with you
I'm back
After so much time
Let me be yours forever
Let me whisper to your soul
All these words
I've kept for you quite long
My only man
I love you.

Regrets

There are so many years
I haven't seen your face
From all I've done I regret only one
That I let you go away
That I wasn't able
To show you how I feel
Through all these years I couldn't speak
Standing so close to you
During these few moment too
When I had a chance for more
I regret also that I stopped to believe
That this love can be real
But now, right here
I call you again, my dear
Much more strong than before
I call you by your name
Because I'm your love
And you are always and again
My man.

No, my love

No, my love
I don't feel any pain in my soul
Even your silence
Is not terrible so much
I just have you Inside
And I feel your light
And now I have this
What I missed so long
Yes my love
I know it's hard
To be with me right now
I know it's even hard to speak but
The most important is
That you are
That you live
And now I'm complete
I can speak again and I feel so great
With you within my soul
Is this love
Can't be real?
I don't believe.

Thoughts

How many times have I played
Here watching thoughts fly by
My soul
I'm here still waiting
For the answer
It's so scary
How easily you could
Crash this world
This world of words
With all my love
To you.

What can I do
That my heart
Can speak like that
Only to you
You are this man
I want to share
My thoughts, my soul
And my body too
You are this man I chose.

Just come back to bed.

I wish to know
Why you don't want
To stop me at all
On this way to you
That I chose
Some time ago
As you know

How do you like
This transmission to your heart?
Could you make love to me
In your dream?

Oh, yes
I want to be undressed
For you today
I want to show you
All these little steps
You could find
To make me feel so fine

Don't you know yet?
What should you do?
I'll show you

So watch me
I'm here waiting
Please come back to bed
Did you forget
How it is nice to be
So in love with me?

Because you were
I remember well
What you can give
To me,
My lovely man

So watch me,
I'm here you can touch
Everything
But please don't hurry up
And try to not forget
About all these
Little parts of me
Which are not always

So hot
Oh, yes I know
How it's nice
To feel your touch
Inside
To feel your lips
So sweet
Every little inch of me
Is hungry

It is so many years
Between us, darling
How do you feel with me?

Right now, right here
What do you think?

Can you tell me your wish?
What can I do for you?

Oh, how it is nice
When I feel your touch,
You know you can ask
And you can get
Whatever you wish
You are my King
So, yes
Don't hesitate and
Come to bed
To me, so bare, so missing
I need your lesson again
I need it so bad
Please come back
I'm waiting for you
My teacher of love.

Can it be just a dream?

My husband is gone
I'm sitting here alone
And I think about you baby.
I'm addicted to you
As you already know
Can this be just a one – way feeling?
With all my passion to you
With all these words too
The ghost inside my being?
I hope it is not like that but
What is the reason
This stillness of you?
Oh baby, this is the longest way
As I ever went to the man
But I'm happy wandering to you so I'll do
But should I?
How I'd like to know
What are you waiting for
Or what are you afraid about
To be with me?
Or maybe...
Your doors are always open
It's just that I can't
Come to your arms again
So simply?
And you are waiting
When I stop to dream
And I'll come to your home
Again, someday...
How I'd like to believe
At this, my sweet
That it's just a time
I need to explain myself
What I feel and what I miss
And then
I just come to you
And you will be pleased
Won't you?

Lesson

My lovely man
It's me again
You know
Today I think
That I really
Need your help
You know
Recently
I can't write
In any other language
Than yours
So, you know
I'm not so good yet
And I really need
Your helping hand
You are an Englishman
So, I think
You could be the best
Teacher to me, I guess
But, the problem is
That I'm not probably
Very smart girl
And, I suppose
This lesson can take
More than a few years
I think even more
Because I'd like to know
A lot about you
And your language too
So please
Help me in this
And teach me long
Teach me strong
Teach me to the end
Of love
But you know
I don't have too much money
Yet to spend
So maybe
I could pay you another way?
What do you think?
About my skin?
One lesson
For one touch
Is it not too much?

Please don't be only a dream

Every day I'm stronger
On this way to you,
More brave more open
But sometimes
I feel so blue
Without you here
And I'm scared
That you and me
Is nothing but a dream
And you will never
Come back to me
You know
I think that these few weeks with you
Mean to me more than everything
This is all I miss
All I believe in
And I have hope for
You are my happiness
And I don't know
What I'll do
If you never let me
Be yours
Don't do this to me

My love
Not again
If you leave me
To drown one more time
In your charm
And you know
That if you only wish
These few weeks
Become eternity

I can't believe

The memory of your eyes
These few words I've heard
When you recently called
Can't make me believe
That you don't care of me
But you are afraid to speak
What does that mean?
Do you love me?
Do you want me?
Why it is so hard
To give me any sign
You know that this time
Is coming
When I wish to meet
You again, my sweet
Are you ready for this?
I hope you wish
The same
I hope you are waiting for me
That I could stay
In your arms
Because I can't come to terms
With the fact
That you
Just gave up.

Just come with me

After years I know
That this world
Is a bit different
Than I thought before
We are all nothing but sinners
And there is nothing wrong in it
We just come and go
We are looking for
These paths
To our own happiness
So, don't be so strong
And come with me
To find a piece of our destiny
Without all these silly thoughts
About what is right or wrong
Because I feel that this way
Means just happy days
For me and you
And this is the only truth
Which should be our way
To the end of our day
So, don't be afraid
To love me again
My wonderful man.

How come you!

How come you never call me again
After all my letters
When I gave myself up to you
On these pages!
How come you are so silent
All the time
Didn't you realize that you are mine?
I stand before you naked
And you, you just stopped
To speak with me at all
What is wrong?
How come you be so strong?
I don't understand
What else I can do
To make you sure
That I'm yours?
Why don't you come on back
To this war, baby
It's just beginning
Don't be afraid
You are this man I mean.

Is it our way to go?

Where is your heaven
My Love?
Is it on this same
Way as mine?
Where is your happiness
My Lover
Is it in this same
Place as mine?
Where is your love
My Man
Is it laid
Inside your soul too?
I'd like to know
How do you find our tomorrow
Do you think we have some chance
To be so happy together again
To laugh and cry
Because we live
And this life
Is just as we dreamt about?

You are mine, don't forget!

I used to live by the rules
Everything or nothing
But this time is different
And I miss even a single kiss
Or just a little sign of your existence
And I'm ready to beg you on my knees
Stay my lover, please

Oh, but my love
I'm afraid
That this way
By these words
I can make you
The most adorable
Man on the world
And it's not what I planned
I'm not sure I'd be glad
Seeing you with another girl
But everything is possible
You are so wonderful
That I'm really scared of you
I'm living so far away
I think I have to move
I should take care of you
There are so many
Beautiful women around
I'm getting to be really afraid of that
You are mine!
Don't forget!
That I need you so bad.

I'm sorry my God.

I'm sorry my God
But I'm not afraid of You too much
I think You are a rather nice Man
So, You can forgive me everything
Besides, I'm not so bad
And all I do, or I'm going to do,
Is just because I love,
And as I know, You like love too
So You can forgive me, I'm sure
But You know that I don't believe too much
In all these church and human and political rights
Yes I know it's only for this,
That we could live in a harmony and peace
But as You know it doesn't work so well at all,
Look at the wars around
But You know, that in the deep of my heart
I like to be free on this way to You, my God
I just want to be happy, that's all,
Do You think I am wrong?
I'm sorry, I don't pray too often
But I know that so many adore You,
So I can love another man this time through
And give him whole this heart I have
Besides You know that I don't like the crowd
And You can even call me a fool
But I don't feel well at the church
So, I hope You don't mind that I don't have faith so deep
And time for singing songs to Your glory indeed
I'm rather busy these days, I'm sorry
I need write to my man another piece,
Besides I have a lot of work at home and around
I need to work for his and other's smiles,
And I don't have the time
For You, too much, but I keep the touch
And You know, that I still believe in You
Sometimes less sometimes more
So, someday I'll come and I hope, You will forgive me too
All these sins I've done or I'm going to do
I have just one ask for You, my Lord
Never let me forget this love
That's all I have, all I care for,
So, just don't let me forget
Please, my God.

Just a waste of the time

Don't you agree
With me
Mon Ami
That we still
Waste the time,
I mean
You and me,
Living at this dream
Only
Do you find my poetry
So fascinating?
I'm not sure
I'll keep writing
Without your
Influence
So exciting.

Why it is so hard

Why it is so hard
To speak with me, my Love
Only because
You waste so much time?
Only because my children
Are not yours?
As they should be
Of course
Only because you forget
To come home
About ten or seven years ago?
I don't know, but why?
You can't even say goodbye?

We are children of the Earth.

Maybe it is just like this
That we are all just children
Playing well in our life
We need some toys, some friends
We play all the time with many games
We win, we lose something, someone
Some plays are dangerous too, some are forever
Some are not funny at all
Especially when we don't have
These toys which we need the most
Or other pupils don't understand that we want to play together
It's hard to say what we should do
To make fun from all this what we do
There is so many plays, so many possibilities
We just need to know, what do we like what do we want
And what we can or not, what we pretend or what we understand
Because there are always some rules
There are always some gods or
The people who seem to be so big to us
So we need to be quite polite sometimes
But don't forget that it is just a life
And we must play well and fair
But whole art is to find
What kind of game or with who do you like play to
So, just make fun, and choose, something useful
Be a doctor, a constructor, be a mother, or the father
Whoever you want to, you can be
Or you can just try to play well at this
What the life brings to you with its fate
Just don't play at war if you don't have to
Because it can destroy the world
Besides it is not funny at all.

I'm sorry, it's you who I miss

You said you are not like this
And when you are with me it means something
One day you wrote that I'm a wonderful lady
And no one should ever hurt me
And yes, my darling
No one had any chance to hurt me anymore
Because it is you who I adore
It is you who I miss and long all my life for
It is you who makes me cry at night sometimes
And it is you who makes me feel alive
I don't know how can I thank you
For all these years when I couldn't stop believing
That you are this man who always will be
Who come back finally and will be this man I want to be with
But you don't know how it hurts when you are alone
When you don't know anything anymore
When you need this touch so much
And you go to feel again
Just a little shadow of this what you've lost
But you know that there is only one, you miss
But you can't find this man who makes you feel like this
I'm sorry that it is you who hurt me so much
Only because you gave me a paradise to touch
And then you have just gone for too long.

I saw the news today

I saw the News today
And I'm really afraid
Because you are there
On this black list
Of al-Qaeda terrorists
I'm not yet, probably
It's because my country
Is not yet rich enough
To be worth of the terrorists' holy bombs
But, my love, this way
I want more that you could stay
At my land for good
I need to protect you
I'd like to hide you somewhere
Maybe at this little town
When we met at the mountains
How I'd like to see you there
Safe and only for me, dear
But if you need to fly
Maybe only to get by,
So all right, I understand
You are the man, but
I spread the coat of love
To protect you forever my boy
I hope you will be fine
Because you are mine.

I'm sorry for you terrorists

This same talk
All the time
And as I see
We have some kind of civil war today
And I hear this terrorist pray:
"You are hard worker,
You are smart,
You have more money, more power, than I
So, you must die"
In the name of God
Of course
Oh, poor people
How you are small
With your mad minds
It is so sad
I'm sorry for you
That you are not smart enough to love
Don't you really know
What is the best in this world?
That you can only make fun
Playing at this war?
With your dirty games
Taking pleasure from the people's fear
What kind of men are you?
Don't you really have
Anything to do?
I'm sorry for you.

Could you?

I can't face all days alone
You are the only love I have ever known
I love this dream to live to
But sometimes it is just not enough
And I wish you could be there
I wish you could be my man again
I want to have you as a lover too
I dream about you
And I decided
So, what do you think about it?
Before I was wrong, to be so slow
And now I know
What I want the best
So, could you
Go with me to bed?
We shouldn't waste another year
We are getting to be old my friend
I think that ten years is enough
To wait for you my love

When I'm in love with you

When I'm in love with you
I feel so strong that I could move the stones
And I feel so good that I could change the world
I'm brave and great that I could play with God
With all my thoughts I keep inside
I feel so special, so fine
And anyone around doesn't know
What is it all about
How wonderful world I see when I smile
Full of hope and desire
Of the new things I could do
Being with you
But when I'm with him
I feel nothing
I don't have a force
And I just want to go
To bed to sleep
I don't need anything
I'm just a little piece of ground
And I don't feel the life around.
I wish to be

I wish to be a perfect woman for you

Yes that's all I want to do
I want to stay your mistress too
That you could take me
In your office the break time through
I'd like to be your lunch
And you know that I taste good
As an orient fruit

And then I'll write another poem for you
To tell you how much I love you
How wonderful a man you are
And if I get well with this
You will touch me so sweetly
And so deeply, that I could
Feel you so good
And then I'll call you
My master

I can be some cleaner lady too
If I could make your bed
At the hotel you stay for a while

I'd like to be your secretary
If you will look at me
And tell me hello in the morning

I could be your little cat too
If you take me to your home
And give me some milk and caress

But the most I'd like to be a little mouse
That you could put me in your pocket
Then I will feel your warmth , so close
And I could see the world by your eyes,
I could go wherever you go, besides
It will be wonderful to me to be like this

But if you want I can be everything you wish
Because I live in your dreams.

What is wrong with us?

It's great that I can
Write to you
Almost every day
I have something to say
But, my love
Do we have any chance
If I'm scared even call to you again?
And you are afraid to call me back
I'm not sure of that
What is wrong with us
Why are we so shy
That we can't just speak
Normally
As everybody does
What is wrong with you?
What is wrong with me?
Where is the end of this story?
Can you tell me now
What are you afraid of?
You know that I'm ready
For a while as well for eternity
So, you don't need to worry
What are you doing tonight
Are you waiting for my sign?
I'm waiting for this the same
So please don't be afraid
And call someday.

Destructive influence

Some very important science meeting today
About the common taxation's programs to repair
I was looking at the tutor with despair
Because I just couldn't concentrate
I see you all the time and talk to you by this line
Right now, my work is just a place
To write for you another piece
About very important things
I don't care about my work anymore
All I need to live for now is just this hope
That you will call me and you will come
How destructive influence
On the Polish science you have
But don't worry about and let's live - the art!

Don't resist

When the woman wants a man so much as I want you
I think you have to know that the world custom is
That you shouldn't resist too much, especially when
You know me and I know too
That I'm not indifferent to you
That you were in love with me
And we have some chance today
I know it was very long time ago, but you are still alone
And I always feel this same
So, stop hesitate and come
Because I'm waiting all the time
For a little sign from your side
Just let me know that you are in love too
And everything will be good
I think that no one ever molested you
The way I do so, be happy and be sure
That I love you.

It's just a tool

It is crazy I know
But if I couldn't write
I'd probably get mad
Seeing you all the time
Inside
And not to act
So I use this site
As a tool
To be with you
Somehow
And now I'm so happy
To know that I'm not alone
Or maybe I'm wrong.

The illusion that you are here

From the time you are here
This place is more exciting to me
So let's play like this
If I can be a little mouse
You can be a child
That's all right too
I want to play with you
I thought I love the man
But now I see
That you are Mr. Mystery
You said you like your site
So, all right
Let's play like this
Let me guess
What do you like the best
I like this home too
I like to play with you
But if our home is this site
So, maybe poetry is our life.

A drug

Suddenly I realised
That I'm going crazy
And this poetry site
Is just a kind of drug
I see more than really is
And I just make a fool
From myself
I don't know what to do now
Who am I?
Who are you?
What I'm doing here with you?
I think I need some rest
To consider if I have a chance
To survive this time
Calling to your heart
Again.

Once we did love

Once
We were lovers
But not to the end
And you have stayed
In my dreams forever
And never I could find
The man like you were
You shouldn't left me like this
So full of hope so warm
If you planned to go so far
But today you are so close again
And all I need is
That you could finish
This what you've started
My friend
I gave you my heart
I gave you my soul
My body is waiting for you
So, what do you need more?

Lost in forest

Sometimes I see you
Wandering among my thoughts
But you disappear quickly
That I can't see you clear enough
Maybe you don't exist
In reality at all?
But I must find you
Someday
If not I'd doubt
In sense of my life
Because nothing
Is the same
And nothing compares
To your hand
To your arms holding me
To your eyes looking here
And your lips talking to me
Because you are everything

And all I need
Is just to feel you again
But there is still
Only a dream
Unreal empty place
Without your face
As a deep forest
I'm walking in
I went here alone
But I want so much
That it'd be you
Who will find the route
Of return
I'm tired, my Love
And I don't have much more force
To go alone
With every moment
I'm just going deeper
To this dream world
But maybe you are
At the next corner
So, I need to wander

Is it really so hard
To find each other?
Where is this man
Who I'm looking for?
Where are you, my Love?

Please be for me

I don't know if you understand this
But I need to be your girl
Please let me do it now
Before I'll tell him goodbye
That's all I ask for
Just let me be yours
Just for a while if you want
But this I'm sure
That I need, I need
I need you more
Than everything I have so far
So, please
There is still a little time
I must wait for you but
I need to come to you soon
Can you understand this?
Will you wait for me?
Please
Be there
When I come
Just wait and...
Smile again
When you see me
That's all I need
For the beginning
Just have a little time
For me
Just a few days
Just a few weeks
That's all I need
All I ask
Will you be there?
When I'll call you
Again?
Please, don't be scared
Don't be afraid
Don't worry
About anything
Just be there
And let me be
Please...

The differences

I'm not sure you feel this little difference
Between these two relationships
Between love and a friendship
Because I feel this very strong
So when you became
So friendly so suddenly
After this time when you were mine
When you were so close
I was completely lost
I didn't know anymore
What to think
And how to speak
To you
So, I was just running away
Seeing you on my way
I couldn't stand
You, so close to me
But with this uncertainty
If you are my friend just
Or you are my man still

But now I'm strong enough
To speak to you, my love
As I always wanted
I'm not afraid anymore
You and me and these
Reality obstacles that exist
Because I wasn't able
To show you
That I can't live
Without you
And that you are always
This man I love the most
And I believe that
You will come back

I lost you my love
Because I loved you
Too much to speak
I think.

I want you here

I want your hands
Put on me
I want your head
On my breast
I want your eyes
Look at me
I want your smile
So sweet
I want your voice
Talk to me
I want your sight
Just be
I need your touch
I need you
Lying by me again
I need to play with
Your blond hair
I need you here
Please come back
To me.

Can you be this man?
Can you be this man?

Maybe you want to know
What I wish from you
My Love
So, what can I say...
Come, watch, touch me
And let me be free
In your arms so sweet

Let me feel and see
My beauty in your eyes
Let me sing
To your heart
This song
Which I kept so long

Let me do what I want
Maybe something more...

I need to know
That you could understand
Every move I would do
Even this not very good
And something else...

I need you could be
The King and the slave
At the same moment

Do you think
You could be like this
To me?

It's quite simple
Look at me

I'm your slave and your Queen
So, for the beginning...
Just take me
In your dream

And then you will see
My castle and my wonder land
And my favourite
Four poster bed

Which is waiting so long
For this night
So special lover's pray
When the King
Returns from his trip
To his Queen
Just don't be afraid
To live in this fairy world
With me

and don't forget to lose your head
If you didn't yet
That's all I wish
And all I demand
From you
My lover man
You don't even need to
Sing a song

It's my job
Oh, I almost forget
That sometimes
I need to dance
With you in the darkened room
With the candles lights on
And I need to feel you
Inside me
After this

So, what do you think?
Could you be this man
I meant?

Hey where are you?

Where are you, my lover
Where Is your home
What do you do these days
Are you alone?
Are you there
In your place still?
Are you with me here
In your dreams?
Do you understand my words?
Do you believe in this song?
Hey, is it you?
Who can read my soul?
Or I'm wrong?
Do you want me at all?
Hey, I'd like to know
Maybe you don't like
Make love in this crowd?
But don't worry about
I'm not very popular so far
How I'd like to know
Your heart and your thoughts
Please let me know
If you are in love
And that you are waiting for me
To come.

We are free here

We can live as we want
We have a freedom
So, you can be my King
And I can be your Queen
My Love
How it's a wonderful world
When you came back
To my land again
And I can sing
This song of love
To you
And I'm so happy to do this
My boy,
So don't be afraid
To use the words like this
Don't be scared to be great
Don't be afraid
To stay The King
You can be everything
If you only believe
In this dream.

The death of love

My love is gone
He is sitting in his armchair
He is drinking a bear
And he is eating his meat
Full of bones to crack it
I can't stand this sound
He is watching TV
I'm in bed sleepy and tired
And I'm dreaming about
The soft music around
And my lost love near me somehow
But the light is too strong
I hide my head deeper in bed
To not hear him to not see the lamp
I'm almost in my dream but
He stopped to watch TV
So I feel he's trying to caress me
From my beck
He wants to take me
But his kisses
Just annoy me
So, I push him away
He try tender again
I don't react I pretend that I dream
So, he stops without any word
He goes to sleep
And in the morning
He is silent and sad
He knows that something is wrong
With us
But sometimes
When I even let him
Take me
I can't stop to think
About the man I love
And I see him above
I don't know what to do
With this fact
That I lost my heart
And I think that
Right now it'd be better
To live alone and dream
About my beloved man
Because everything else

Is without any sense
And because I love
To live this hope that
He will be back
He lives in all my thoughts
He is my favorite topic
To talk
He is inspiration to my write
He is actually everything
What I have inside
And this what make me smile
He wins with everything
He wins with the reality.

Still waiting for the king

Some of us can give our hearts very fast
Some just wait for the special occasions
Others don't care of love at all
And how it is with me?
I'm waiting for my King
Who I've met once and he is the owner of my heart still
And all I can give to others now
Is from this time just a shadow of me
Because all I have inside is given to this guy
I've met once and only he is this King
Who I was looking for very long
And I couldn't find again
No one who compares, so I wait
That he come back to me
Because I'm his Queen
And I believe that
He'll be happy with me.

What is this write actually

This writing is a kind of experiment
I'm open more than I even want
But I'm scared that this way
I can lose you forever
Even before I really get you
My Love, but
If I don't I'll be sure
That it is you
And you will be sure of this too
If you won't be scared of my thoughts
And my love to you
Then you can be this man
Who would stay with me for good
If you only listen this
What I have to say to you

But now you know
That if you won't be a good lover
I can even tell this to another
Is it not terrible to you?
I hope you are strong enough
To not care of this too much
I hope that you are
Really open minded
And you know
That I like this risk
A little bit
So, now I can lose
My job, my husband
And the worst - you too
But what can I get?
Real love and myself
So, I think it is worth it
Besides I like this talk
I love to feel the contact
With you and with the world
I think that it is even the way of living
I'm just not sure yet
I could make money off it
I never tried to sell myself
And these thoughts I have
And if anybody is interested
This kind of dream to get
Maybe it is the best what I could do
But I'm not sure I'm good seller at all
And is it easy to handle all of my dreams

To live from this but only with you
It is just another dream I have
Or it could be truth
Who knows?

You know that I don't need
Real work to live
I prefer to have
This free time to think
To realize myself
I don't need to be
The business woman at all
I would write and paint
And that's all I could do
But I'm not sure
If I'm able to get by this
So, I try to be a scientist
But I don't feel this
And I don't think so
I could be good engineer at all
I don't like to built the road
I prefer to write about my Love
And measuring this ground
Is not so interesting as your heart
I feel you inside my soul
And all I want is
Talk to you about this
What my heart whisper to me
And that's all my life I think
But what if inspiration's will hits
After we meet?
Probably I'll find something else
To live
I don't know why
But everything you do now
Looks for me very attractive
So, maybe I'll try to work with you?
Will You take me to your crew?
I don't know
I think I did everything wrong
To be with you
My Love, but maybe not?
You are still silent
So, I don't know
But this is exciting too
So, everything I can do
Is just go to you and check
Someday

Because you can't speak
From this time I opened my heart
To you
You didn't say yes
You didn't say no
What should I think about this?
I don't know
But you know that I believe
At you still
So, I need to go
Just wait for me, my Love
But what if you are just scared of me?
What I'll do then?
I don't know
I'll try to understand this
I'll try to built my world again
And still live some how
But this is what I'm afraid about
The most right now.

I try to play

I try to play
But it's not a game
Because I really love
I try to do something with me
But you are the only one I see
There is not any world anymore
And I don't care
About anything else
I just want
To be with you
Again.

I don't need your words at all

All right then
Don't say any word
Just be there
When I'll come
I don't need
Your words at all
I prefer your touch
I just want
Your love
But if you can't
Offer me that
Give me back
My broken heart.

A very simple dream

I had very simple dream today
I'd like to built a home
Real house in the place
Which we find the best for us
The most beautiful
I'd like to live with you there
And care for you, for children
And for this house too
It's strange dream to me
Uncommon because
I was rather scared to live there
I was afraid this kind of simple life
But now I dream about this home with you inside
So tender, so sweet and so real
Would you like to share the life with me?
Someday?

I know it a lot of words I gave to you

I know it is a lot of words
I'm giving you, my love
Maybe you were not ready
For this but
I just want to show you
That you are this man who
I love and this is my way
To you
Because I know now
That you are this one
Who I really want and
I'm doing what I can
To be your woman again
I hope you understand

If I know that you it's you
You should know this too
And any poem cant change this
And you are always ready
To be with me
That's all I want to believe.

No, don't be friends

No, my love
Don't be friends
We could destroy
Everything again
No, I don't need
Another friend
I want you as a man
Are you ready for some change?
I want to play with you
At this game
I want to wait
In the darkened room
For your hand
I want to see
Your silhouette on me
In the mirror
Which is hanging above
In my dream
I want to feel your frame
Trembled when you touch me
I need to feel your tender fingertips
Wandering slowly,
Upward, inward
Of my body
I need you like this
Please come again
I miss you, my only man.

A delicate case

It's a case very delicate
I want you
But I know as well
That pressuring you too much
I can scare you away
And this way
I'll lose my heart forever
Because so far
I was just keeping you
Inside as a treasure
But I've never tried
To stand face to face
With this case
And now
I can't wait
Because I realized
That I just
Waste the time
Dreaming all my life.

Dream

I want a big house
I want to listen the music around
I want to play with my thoughts
I want to dance
I want to wait
For you inside
I want to see the ocean down
I want to take a bath
Naked delighting in the waves
Which are caressing me in the sun-rising light
And I want to come back
To our great bed
When you are just waking up
My Man
I love you then
And you are
With me again.

I'm just coward of love

You know
That writing to you
Is much more simple
Than standing face to face
With you, my Love
And be still
So self confident
I'm afraid of this
And I'm scared more than you
But soon I'll do it
Yes, you can be sure

Don't be silent your whole life

What do you want
What do you wish
Why it is so hard to speak with me
You were such an open boy
When we met
And what happened with you today
Where is your lovely voice
So sweetly whispering
To my soul
I need to know
What do you think
About me
After years
Don't be so silent
All your life, please
Because it is hard to me
To live with this uncertainty.

Can you forgive me now?

It's all because
You were so scared
This unborn child
That we could have
You shouldn't stop
Putting your hands on me
So suddenly
You shouldn't
Become so responsible
You shouldn't
Say that you like me
And that you always will
You shouldn't stay here
To start build this dream
You shouldn't call to me maybe
After some time
You shouldn't be silent
After all these letters I wrote
You made me this way shy enough
To never have the chance
To say to you all the truth
That I always wait and
I can't stop loving you
You shouldn't build your own world
You shouldn't have left me alone for so long
But you've done
But please don't be scared of me
Right now
I'm this same girl as you know
I didn't come to fool you
And I hope you understand that I must
Try again to start with you this life
I shouldn't marry him maybe
But I did
Can you forgive me?

I wasn't so strong

Honey, maybe you are
Strong enough to live like that
But I couldn't stand
These lonely nights
But I wasn't brave enough
To knock again on your door
Besides you forgot
To leave me your new address
So, how could I come
When I had enough to be alone?

How it's sad (be careful it's about sex)

Do you know that no one
Never has got me
On the floor
No one tried to do it
At work
I've never been taken
On the chair, on the table
On the stairs, on the desk
Any top of the mountain
Any roof on the high building too
Never has a chance to see
Me and you
Doing such things, though
How it's sad
That no one has got me
There yet.

It's just a moment I need to realize that you are just a dream I have.

It was so long ago
But I still feel you
So strong, so clear
And I don't know
How it is that
I just can't forget
This while
And I even can't
Imagine how could I live
Without this dream
I remember so well
Every smile and gesture
Every touch and word
But you know
That it was so long ago
And maybe I need yet
A little more time
To realize
That it should
Stay like that
And you and me
It's just a memory
Is this what you want?
To stay just in my mind?
All right, but why I must cry?
The sweetest boy
Why I must miss you so much,
But if you decide
To stay like that
I'll live with you
Just inside
Because this one
I'm sure now
That you are the part of me
And you must live here
Forever
As a gift, as a treasure
As a cause of my tears
And the deepest pleasure.

Let this dream come true

I just have hope that I'm not
A kind of Polish folklore to you
(I don't like folklore at all)
I don't know why I had to choose
Such a hard man to love but
I just love you and I don't know
What to do now with my heart
Which is describing this story
Of my life
You know that I always liked
To write something
I used to write before
I do anything
And you must to know that
Most of this what I write
I have in this real life
So, right now it's just
A little time we need to
Make this dream come true
Because I believe in you
And in my heart too.

Is it something wrong with me?

Do you think I'm silly or mad
Because all I remember
From student time
Is just one night
When I was dancing
With my friend
And all what I want to remember
From all my life
Are just these
Few days and nights
When I had a chance
To be with you
My Lover man
Do you think
It's something
Wrong with me?
Please tell me.

Maybe this dream is all you need

I live in my memories of when
I'm here with you, my man
Just sometimes I'm not sure
I want you more for real
Or only in this dream
Because this way
I have you even more
Than I probably ever could
In this real life
So, I can't decide yet
Is this dream just a waste the time
Or not at all,
Or something much more
I'm here with you
So sweetly, so complete, so free
And this is great to me
You know?
Maybe it is just another dimension
That is perfect for you and me
To live in
And we can do here
What ever we want
Yes mon Ami
I want this dream
Maybe even more than you
For real
I can play with you here
And maybe it is enough to me
But... what do you think?

What are you going to do with me now?

You were this man
I had to know
To believe in love
But you got away baby
For so many years
To stay alone
With all these things to do
But you forgot
About this little case
To close,
So, now I'm standing here
Asking you for this
That you could tell me
What you are going to do
With me
When I love you still
And you are this man
Who I can't never forget.

I shouldn't ask anything

Who am I?
I'm the woman
Married mother of the two
Beautiful boys
That aren't yours
So, what am I looking for?
What can I offer to you now
My Love
I wasn't strong enough
To wait for you
So long
And now I shouldn't ask
Anything from you
I know, you are so wonderful
It's not important how I feel
I don't have the right
To be your girl
Yes, I think
That you deserve
For someone better
Than I could be
Because I've done everything
To him not to you
As I should.

I'm so scared I let you feel not how I planned

How I'd like to know
Why you are so silent, my love
I wish to know your thoughts
I don't want to be intrusive
Within your world
So, please tell me
What should I do
Because I'm not sure
If I'm welcome now
In your home
I was so loud
Maybe you don't like
When someone is talking to you
This way I do
But you know
After so many years
I have a lot of to say to you
But I wish to know
How do you feel right now
Please try to tell me
Because I'm getting to be
So scared again
That I did something wrong
And I make you feel
Not as I want
It was just to let you know
That you are still this man I love
Don't forget that I'm not an angel
And I know that you are not as well
But the problem is that
I still love you and I miss you
More than everything

So, don't be so silent, please
I can forgive you everything
You have done or even this what you didn't
I just love you that's all, my dear.

Do you read me?

How I wish to know
Do you read me or not
It's so sad to me
When I think
That all I do
Is just nothing to you
And perhaps
You don't even find any time
To look
What I have to say to you
How it's hard to think like this
How it's sad to not believe
That someday you'd be with me
I'm not sure I could live
Without this hope anymore
It is growing inside me quite long
These thoughts embedded deep
Within my soul, and now
This dream becomes a part of me
And I can't even imagine
How could I live without it.

My life is so beautiful from the time I found you

My life is so beautiful
From this time I found you
You belong to me
I see your face around me
I feel you in the air
I find the sight of you everywhere
In every tree and stone
On the grass and the rocky hill or
During the sunny day and in the rain
All the Earth has the smell of you
That I can touch by my thoughts
And it's so wonderful to feel you there
My life becomes so real again
I'm going all the years through
Taking delight from these sweet memories of you
I can feel you at the present things I do
And I can dream about these wonderful days too
When we will start to share our life and I know
That I couldn't live without you anymore
Even just inside my soul, yes my love
I'm waiting again and I hope
That someday you will come
And thanks to you I set free
My heart and my soul
And now this life becomes so bright
You let me be for you like that
I was missing this such a long time,
I think you know that
I'm like a bird that need this song
To feel free and alight within my heart
So, thank you for that, my love.

I wish to know your habits

I wish to know
Your daily habits
You live alone, so
You must like something
And dislike too
I wish to know
All of these
Little things
You do
I wish to be
Someone who can
Understand the man
As you are, my friend
I wish to know
Your thoughts
And desires
And your silence
I think I can
Forgive you
Everything you could do
And I wish to know
How it is with you.

Do you know the cure for love?

Do you know the cure for love?
Can you find a way
To stop thinking about you
During these whiles
When I make love to him
Not to you, for example?
I can't set free away myself
From these thoughts
I can't feel his arms anymore
I belong to you
Within my soul
And I don't know what to do
I just want to be with you
But at this same time
There is nothing what scares me so much
Than the possibility of you touch.

It's great to be on the same side

It is so nice
To be on the same side
Of Europe as you are
But the real Union
I will feel
When my Englishman
Will come to me
But it's great, by the way
That we can pass the borders
Without any problems anymore
It's a bit like in this old song
Which everybody knows
„Imagine there is no countries..."
It's wonderful to see
How imaginary slowly becomes real
And this vision of perfect world
Is here where we live, my love
So interesting life starts to be
When we are so open
To this world
So different and similar
at the same time
I love my own land
If I can go wherever I want
Because I need free space to live
And one country is not enough I think,
To live we need all Earth

Little fears

I'm afraid that
I'm not interesting enough
To stay with you too long
I'm scared that I wouldn't be
Such perfect lover as you dream about
I remember myself from this time
When you were angry with me
That I wasn't as you wanted I'd be
I'm so scared that someday
You could look at me
And I wont see love in your eyes
I'm afraid
I wont be this girl right
Do you know that
The power of my love to you
Strictly depends
Of my self-confidence
And through these days
When I'm weak in my eyes
I'm afraid the most this love
I can love you only
When I believe in myself
That's why it was so hard
For me to show you how I feel
Through so many years
I preferred to be with someone else
You are too strong for me sometimes
And I resign but then I feel
That what is left is just a shadow of me
And this real life which I need to feel
So, that's why, I fight right now
And I hope that this time I win
Not with you but with myself.

Do you believe we could be together in real?

I'm here watching
The stars, the trees
The clouds, the babies
Thinking about this
What has happened
Some time ago
What is right now
And what can be
How wonderful life is
When I have my past
How could I live
Without my memories
I'd be so empty and so tired of all these things
Which happen through all days in present
Who I'd be without my dreams about you?
Just a simple girl in the little part of this Earth
I can't even imagine myself this way
You were always here, even before
We have met, my love
I was dreaming about you
About the man wandering
Around the world
Who will find me here
And then we will live together
Taking pleasure from each other
Yes, you were this man
I was dreaming about all my life
And you stayed like that
Just in my mind
But I still believe
That we could live
In reality too
Do you believe at this
Mon amour?

How it's nice Mr. Blair

How it's nice from your side
Mr. Blair that you decided
To open your door
For the Polish workers to go
To your country
I'm so proud of you too
My lovely English man who I know
That you are from
The country like this
And you know that
There is not very important
How many people
Would work there or here
But much more brilliant is
These possibilities
That some of us can just try
To go and fight
On this common war
For a better job and the life
Or just to go to know
That we can try to live and find
Something interesting
At the foreign land
Just for adventure and the joy
Of life
And for this wisdom
Which is coming
From the difference
Between you and me
How it's a great decision
Mr. Blair
I really appreciate it
And I think
That someday
I'll try to go
To find some job too
To be sure
That I'm good
So, thank you Mr. Blair
What else I can tell you
It was nice to hear
Such news today.

Girl go to France for a little romance

Girl if you don't feel well
With this place you live in
And the men around
Aren't as you dream about
Let's go to France
For a little romance
And then you will feel
As a natural woman again
Because of this
Plaisir d'amour which
In this lovely wine's flowing country is
Yes I know this and I can recommend
Frenchmen are great
They know how to speak
They know how to kiss
They know every woman needs
They know where to go for a dinner
They have such delicious cuisine
And this wine which is so
Delightful aphrodisiac to feel more
From this lovely cheerful kiss of simple love
Yes, girl if you don't feel well with the place
You live in, go to France, even for a while
To believe in yourself and in the men again
I would stay there I'm sure
If I hadn't lost my heart before.

How to not lose this pleasure

Sometimes I think
There is nothing funny
In this world to me
There is nothing special to play with
I don't have the force to live
I'm a little isolated from you today
But I don't want to go away
What to do with myself
To make life more real
To be more consequential
To be sure that I can do whatever I want
And not lose this pleasure at all
What to do with my mind
To not be scared of the fight
No fear to lose the feelings of being in love
When I feel something like that
What is not possible to describe.

Internal fight

Sometimes I think
I don't need any work to live
I find myself too soft for this fight of a better place
In this world
I prefer to give up before the start
And live a little outside
But after some time I need to prove to myself
That I'm not so weak
To not try to take a part in this life's war
And then I'm going again
As everybody does to this place
When I need to show how many skills I have
So far, how good or brave I'm
To not resign from any challenge I find on my way
I balance between
The weakness and the power I have within,
Between the death and the life
Because sometimes
I'm losing the sense of this
All these things and I'm not sure
if I want to play my role still
In this beautiful world
Because I don't have the force
To be so fantastic woman
To all of you and to myself too
I don't have the force and wish
To proving myself that I'm good
So good as I maybe should

"Just love yourself"
You can say, yes it's great advice
But it's not so easy sometimes
I'm still working on this
But there is always like a wave
When I believe and don't believe
In myself
And this is how the life looks like
When the woman is unsure of her charm
When the man doesn't make her sure
That she is cute and wonderful
And she think that it is all she needs
To be happy, beautiful and cool
To feel comfortable and satisfied in this world.

How it'd be dark without all of us

Maybe it's good to know
That you are not
The smartest girl in the world
That there is always some better one
Than you are but there is not the reason
To worry about
It's great that you can
Always learn something
From others
That's why they are for
All people of this world
It's good to not count
For them too much though
If you look for things this way
It's always such a nice surprise

If someone gives you smiles
If someone tries to help you

With some things you have to do
But you are not good enough,

Then you can smile
To see how wonderful this world can be
When you don't expect too much
And you get more than you imagined

How this earth would be sad
Without all these sweet people around

How it would be empty
Without these ones
Who have something to say to us

How this world would be dark
Without the light

How it could be ugly and boring
Without all these monuments which
Some of us can built

I love to see this world so rich
Even if I can't touch
All of these things
That the life brings
And this is the way I like to live
Sometimes just watching
And learn all the time

How to be better one a bit
To know more to have a choice
And to find the best way to go.

All you can do here

Watch, learn and feel
Then teach and use your skills
That's all you can do
In this world I suppose
And play well of course
Not charge anyone too hard
Not even yourself, you can't do that
You would forget to smile
And this is unforgivable, besides
It's not a good way of life
You never know the whole story
So, you can be wrong, I'm sorry
But I think it's better for you to realise
That the things are not black and white
And the truth is mostly
In the middle of this route
Which you can call wrong or good
And don't forget that you can be free
Only if you know enough
To have some choice and even then
You can't be so sure
If you are right or wrong
But don't worry about and smile
That's the way it is and this is fine
Oh, there is one more thing
Don't let yourself be used more than
You use someone else
You must balance between
This situation when
You can be up or down
Because, as you know,
You are not alone in this world
So you must learn all the time
How to live with people around
Just balance, and play well
This is not the hell, besides
You don't need to be friends with all of them.

Just yes or no

Why you can't say
Any word, my Love
Just yes or no
For example?
I'm not so sure now
I'd go to you
If I don't know
You want to see me at all
I want and you know
But of course
I understand
It's hard to decide
You don't want to
Crash my world but
You know that I want this
So, stop resist, please
And take me as I wish
Don't tell that you are afraid of me
I'm such a nice girl
Yes sometimes a little sad but
Maybe just because
You are still outside
So if you only come back
I won't be like that
I promise.

All because of...

If you wouldn't want me
I'll think that it's just
Because of my small breasts
So, you shouldn't let me go in
This complex, Darling
You know I'm so pretty girl
Looking for all
Besides it's not so important
I love you, and it should be
Exciting to you enough
To take me, don't you agree with me?
Tell me that you love my small breasts
Please
I need to know this that you accept
My lovely complex too
And that you love me all
Even when
I'm too shy sometimes
Or when I can't find a way
Or when I don't know what to say
Even then when I say too much
I know it's not a good way
To fascinate the man
Talking about such things
You know I'm not a sex bomb type at all
But I have something more
Big heart to you, my Love
And besides I'm funny girl sometimes too
Is it not enough?
How I wish to know.

I wish you here

I wish you were here
My lovely dear
I wish you could take me
To our secret place
In the mountains' alley
I wish you lay by me
I need you to touch me
I wish to take your head
With my fingertips
I wish you were with me
I wish you touched me there
I wish you could run
Your fingers along my back
I wish you kissed me
on my neck
I wish to feel your lips
I wish you could find the way
Inward me
I wish your hands
I wish your touch so bad
I miss you my lover man
I miss you as no one else
I wish we could go farther
Inside of us
I wish to know
What means the real orgasm
I wish my Lover
Come back to me
Not only in my dream.

I don't see the reason why

Every day I fall in love
With you again
Every day I wish more
To be your woman
Even if I know
How sad can be the end
I can't find the way
To put you behind me
My Englishman
I don't even try
To set free my heart
Should I?
I don't see the reason
Why?
Should I stop
Loving you
Inside
Only you can be
This one
Who decide
What should I do
With my heart.

Yes or no I wish to know

My dearest man

I wish to know
Do you want me or not
I need to know
Do you love me or not
Yes or no
Yes or no
I want to know
Do you want that
I'll come to you or no
Yes or no
Yes or no
I must know
I wish to know
I need to know
or I don't?

Do I really want this?
Or maybe I'm afraid
What your answer can be
Or maybe
That the charm will splash
As a bubble
I'm afraid to lose
What I have now with you
All these hopes and dreams
But also I'm so scared that
Anything won't be right
When we finally meet
That I just won't know
What to do standing by you
Maybe I'm afraid of this more than
Your answer "no"
But I still want to know
And I'm scared of this too
I just don't know what to do
But I need to know
How I get on you
By my words
Please give me some sign
Just a little point
Just yes or no.

It's just I need to know if you wish the same, my love

To this day I can't understand
Why we have never
Made love to the end
You said you don't want
To hurt me this time
When you were mine
But I know now that this
Doesn't hurt at all
Now I know that lack of this hurts much more
And dreaming of you was sometimes hard
Especially when we lost contact
And I was not sure if I'll ever see you

I've never had a chance to feel the same to another man
And I miss this night all my life
But I can't, I couldn't do anything so far
To arrange a new meeting with you

I was just not able to do it
I'm still afraid to meet you
But you, why you were always so passive too?
You seemed to be so happy seeing me every time
But you have never tried to do something
To make me more sure about this what you want
You haven't done anything
To give me a little more assurance, my Love
You are impossible
And now I'm still at the beginning
Of this way to you

But this time I hope I won't run away
Seeing you on my way
And you know much more
About this love
Which I was hiding so long
Which I even tried to throw out
From my heart
But everything in vain

I love you again
I don't care of the world's rules
I don't care about anything at all
Nothing is wrong in love
But it's just I need to know
If you want this too, that's all.

I'm ready for love

I don't know the end
This story of love
But now
When you are so close
To touch
When I know
I can see you again
I just can't
Forget that it is you
Who should be my man
My lover from dreams
Please come back to me
I'm waiting for this time
With all my passion
And all my desire
Which I was keeping
Only for you
And now I'm ready
For this love
To start a new chapter
Of my life
There was the time
I was a good wife
But now I need
Something more to live
I need you, my lover
I want you, my man
It's you who make me feel
So natural a woman again
When I think of you
My heart is singing
That's why I want
To be your girl
So, please come back to me
And tell me your every wish
I'm ready to do everything.

I just hope you are happy with me

How I wish to know
Are you happy with me
or not
I just want to be yours
And I'm writing this song
Do you think it's wrong?
To say to you what I want
That I'm still in love with you
And about this night too
I didn't mean to confuse you, my love
Don't forget, I gave you so many chances
To say no, to tell me that
I shouldn't maybe go this way
But you became silent
And I'm not ready yet
To check
Will you answer
My phone
Or not
But we have still a little time
To wait
So I just hope
You are happy with me
My Love.

Are you confused over me darling?

Are you confused over me, darling?
I know you want to be the right man
But what to do in the situation like this
When the woman wants you and misses you
And this way that means "proper"
Can be just a great disappointment to her?
You are in a trap I know but
You didn't know you find on your way
19 years old virgin anyway who had dreamt
About the man as you were
So, now you see what can be
With the little girl I use to be sometimes
I'm a bit older right now
And much more open for you but
This what I try to do
Doesn't sound right to you
But how to refuse such an offer?
I know that you don't know
What to do with me now
My Love, but I just have a hope
You don't charge me too hard
And that you know I'm real to you
In everything I say and I ask for.

Men be careful for young girls

Men be careful
For young girls
They can find you
After years
They become poets
And then they write a lot of poems
To you

And then you don't know
What to do
With such a woman
As she is for you

And now you have to pay
Your rent because you are still
The most wonderful man to her
You must pay
For all these years
When she was dreaming
About your comeback

And now you must read
All these words of love
She has been keeping for you
So long

And right now it's hard to decide
What to do with such a girl
Who wants you so much still
But she is able only to write.

A thousand words

I can tell you a thousand words
I can write poems too
But I don't know
How can I speak to you
That you could
Want me the same way I do
Thousand of words from my side
And your silence so far
But just one phone call is enough
And I know
That you are just you
Who I belong to
So, what else I can do?
To show you that I love
And that there is no way
To me, just you
And this way I go
Until we meet
My sweet boy.

Please don't be kind

Please don't be just kind
And tell me what you really want
If you don't need me
Just say no
Because I'm going to be mad
Without you here
But with this hope
For you still
I can't live normally

I'm hungry for you
And I don't know
What to do with myself
I'm so sad
Please I can't live in
Just this hope
So long
I need you
So bad
Please come back
Or tell me
That I shouldn't
Miss you
Because your heart
Is cold

I feel I'm dying
From this love
But I can't
Leave you alone
I just can't.

There is no point

I wish to go to your fairy Island
I want to see the place
You lived as a child
But there is no point
To go there alone
Don't you know?

Yes I'd like to have
A wonderful house too
Someday I'll do it but
There is no point
To live there alone
But with you, my love.

We have to finish this somehow

It is so long ago,
We haven't seen each other
Maybe I'm silly to think
That you are alone still
It's natural
You have had a lot of girls after me
And now, you are scared
What do I want
From you after years
But why you can't
Just tell me
That I should stop this?
Maybe it's easier to wait
For the end
Maybe she stops by herself
You are right I shouldn't be like that
I'm just ridiculous I know
I don't know
What happened with me
I'm sorry
I shouldn't love you still
After so many years
I shouldn't love you
We've never ever been a couple
You were no one to me
I was no one to you
Just a simple lovely
Few days that's all

How could I forget
That it is just like that
It's normal, natural it's fine
I'm just an idiot sometimes
Romantic bly bly

How should I forget
How the life looks like in real
Love, love, love
What is that mean?

Can I love you
We never ever lived together
We don't know too much
I'm just silly I know
Girl with too big imagination

Yes, maybe you are right
Maybe it's just crazy
And I should give it up
No, it can't be like that
We could spend some wonderful time
But maybe not at all
Maybe you are afraid of me

No, I shouldn't go to you
But will you come to me?
I don't think so
It's just hopeless, you know?

I never thought
I'd be so piteous
I think I leave it now
I don't understand
Why I still love you
Could you stop looking at me
When I make love to my husband,
Please?
How do you think I can be to satisfy
When I can't stop
Seeing your face above?
When I can't stop talking to you
In my thoughts?

You know it was always like that
Before I met some boys too
And I could spend with them some nice time
But I always have seen you inside

You are impossible
I can't forget you
You are still
The most wonderful boy
In the world

If you can't be mine
Could you stop being so fine?
Maybe tell me something not nice
Maybe tell me that
You love somebody else
Just do something
Because I can't stop
Thinking of you

It's not natural to live

Like that
We should finish this somehow
I need to know
Your feelings
I need to know
Do you want me or not

I need to know you
What happened to you
Mon Amour?
Don't you really have
Anything to say
After this year?

Just stay where you are

I don't know, my Love
We will be together or not
But one I'm sure
From this time I've found you
I feel that I live again
And I'm so glad
That I have a kind of contact
With you
And this is enough
To be happy
Violently happy, my Love
Because it's sometimes so hard
But please don't go anymore
So far away from me
I need to know
Where are you, my friend
Don't disappear again
I'm asking you of this
Even if you can't be with me for real
Stay like this and try to be my friend again
Try to speak with me sometimes
Maybe you need more time
I don't know, but just stay where you are
And I'll be fine, to know
That you are still on the range
I love you I accepted this fact
And I feel all right

Invitation

Come inside me
I want this so hard, Darling
Please come inside

Could you touch me there?

Could you touch me
There?
And here...
And here...
And here yet
Oh yes
And don't forget
About this...
And there...
And here...
And here yet...
Oh it's wonderful
And here...
Here...
Yes
A little more yet
Please
And here...
There...
Yes
And there...
And here...
Here...
Oh, don't forget
About my little finger yet
Oh, my Sweet Boy
You are just wonderful tonight
Let me touch you now...
Let me kiss...
Yes I wish...

Don't be afraid to love me

How it is easy for me to say to you
This simple words
I love you

That was so clear to me
From the start
When we met
And it is still this same
My heart is telling you
I love you

Such simple words
But it is a little sad to me
That you never believed
That I'm real
Why?

Only because I was too young?
Only because you had your plans?
Only because you didn't understand
Why it was hurtful to know
That you must go
Or maybe because you were too busy
To want me, and my love
But what do you think now?
Please don't be afraid of this love
Don't be afraid to love me
My sweet honey boy
Love is good, love is real
Love is this magic you can feel
Don't worry about anything just be
Again with me, it's so easy, so clear
Please be with me for real
I have a lot of patience to you
You have a lot of patience to me, as I see
So, maybe it's good sign, don't you think?

This moment when I knew

I have to get my days through
With or without you, I'm never sure
During this grand silent space
Without your voice, without your face
Are you my man?
Or it was all nothing but dream
About true love within
The whispers in my mind
Reminds me of our meeting still

You are the one I most loved
At the first sight when I saw your face
or maybe at the second one
After my short silly trip
When I couldn't stop thinking of you
And that I just have to see you again
Or maybe when I found you at this school
And I saw you and your smile so bright
Yes it was this moment, when I knew
That you are the one I love.

What are you waiting for

I wish to know
Your heart and your thoughts
I wish to know your dreams
I wish to know all your needs
All your fantasies
I wish to know what do you want

I wish to know
What are you waiting for
What do you feel
Looking on this site
Looking at me
Are you waiting for that
I could realize again
That I'm alone
With all my love
To you,
My Friend?

I wish to know
Did I go wrong
To write like this
Maybe you don't feel well
With such things
Sharing me and my love to you
With the world
I'm scared this too
Perhaps I shouldn't send
The messages to your work
Maybe I shouldn't tell
My friends that I love you
But what the friends are for?
Don't you know
How it's hard to understand
Why you are so silent.

Pick up the phone please

Please, my love
Don't be sorry
Of all these years
We have had lost
I know you never
Meant to break my heart
I try to understand
You had to go but
Now, please
Don't be afraid
Pick up the phone
When I'll decide to call
To start this new age
With you
Don't be sorry of the past
Maybe we needed this time
To understand a few things
But now, now
We could start again
So, please don't hesitate
Don't worry about me
Even a while with you
Is worth more than everything in this world
Please don't let me destroy this again
Don't let me find another lover, my man
I want to be with you
Because it's you who are my love
Even if for a while
It's worth
Please wait for me then
Prepare your bed
Show me your place
And be my man again
This is all I want
From you, all I expect
Give me this
Give me yourself
And this holy while with you
Which I could remember
To the end of my days
I'm ready even to die
After this night
But before
I just wait for you
My Love.

Sad advice

Someone just gave me
Advice this morning
It makes me sad but
Maybe he is right
Let's see what I received :
"If you love something
Set it free,
If it comes back to you,
It's yours
If it doesn't
It never was"
It's hard, you know?
It's hard to realize
That you just
Don't love me
I want to cry
Seeing this advice
But maybe he is right
So, you never were mine?
How it's hard
To believe this
How it's sad but
Maybe he is right
I should set you free
My Love
As I've done before
Maybe someday
You will be back
To me again
I'll live this hope
To the end
But don't worry about me
I'll be fine I think
I'm sorry
If I was wrong,
My Love.

Desert

desert
time is going
quickly
slowly
some things
to do
to control
make a coffee
dinner
TV
suddenly
something happened
excitement
talk
hot
high
feel
strange
smile
the end
desert
little things
around
dreams
life
hope
for the next
feelings wave
in the air.

Mr. Traveller

I know it was just a while
But so intensive
So far
I didn't feel
Anyone else
And now
It is just a hunger
Inside
For something real
For something strong
Something special
What was so close
I don't like it
I don't like
Lost chances
This time
It wasn't my fault
This time
It is you
Who went out
Before real start
To miss
Everything
I don't like it
I know it wasn't my choice
And I can't do too much
But it's just
The last word I can say
For the end
I don't like it
I know we even
Haven't seen each other
But I don't like it
When the man who seems to be
This guy right
Is such a coward
By the way
Mr. Traveler
What are you looking for
In this world
If you afraid
Love.

Cold inside

When I'm not in love
I feel this special sadness
Inside
When I start again
To be with the man
But I need to be a woman
So I go to another
Who makes me feel this way
And for a while it's OK
But this sadness inside
Is still racking my heart
To the end
Of the new romance
With the man
I'm not in love
I can't love anymore
If I know
That the man
I wish to be with
Is so close but silent
And
In the deep of my heart
I'm still with him
In my dream
Lying with husband
Trying to love a new one too
Always this same
Sadness of the heart
After another cold night
Cold inside.

Wicked game

You said that
I don't hurt you
This way
You don't love me
Then...
So, it's just
A wicked game
Between the woman
And the man
I understand
And you know
I'm not sure
It's sad at all
It's just a different
Kind of me
Which likes this play
With you and me
And this cold love
In the hotel room
Where I know
I can do
What ever I want
And you too
Because it's just a play
Between the woman and the man
Who understand.

Yes I said goodbye

Yes I said goodbye to you but it doesn't mean that
I stopped to dream about your lovely face
About this perfect romance
About me in your arms
Yes I love you still
You are this right man to me
I wish to spend the night with you
I wish to be yours

Yes I've got married when you have been gone
But it's not a reason to not say any word
Besides romance is very common here
So, don't be afraid too much
I can't set free my heart from you
No one else is so cute
What can I do
I wish, I wish to be yours

I don't understand why
Why you are afraid even speak
What's wrong with me now
That you can't
Hey, where is this man
In you
I met once
Don't waste this time
We could spend together
Just come for a while
You know what I want
Just take me
My love
And then
You can go
If you must
But don't leave me like that
Without any word
Without any sign
It's not right.

And then maybe you will speak with me again

I understand that
You don't want romance
So, this summertime is lost but
It's not the end
I have had enough time
To realize
That I'm not in love
With my husband anymore
I'm cheating him in my thoughts
Long enough to be sure
That if I love someone
This man is you
Besides I think I need the rest
From this family life, so
Maybe it's time to ask him
For freedom
I think it's without sense
To stay in this marriage spend
Which is just a silence
Between me and him
Two separate worlds we live in
Which no one even try
To understand
I know it can be hard
Because of the children
We have
But if we stay friends
We will be also their parents
To the end so
Maybe it's not so terrible at all
To live apart
What do you think about this
My Love
Then I find a great job
And move to this town
Where you live in
And then
Maybe you will speak with me
Again.

I'm sorry that I'm happy

I'm sorry that
I'm so happy
Because of this
What I heard some time ago
That you are not married
That you are alone
I know that the single life
Is not too healthy
For the man
For no one I suppose but
Maybe it mostly depends
From the second side
So, maybe you were right
To stay like that
My husband for example
Can he be happy now
When he knows
All these thoughts
I have had so far
From all this year
I'm not sure
I know that I hurt him but
I must say this
I'm happy too
That he knows this
And he's touched
I know it sounds terrible
I'm possibly kind of sadist but
I'm glad he knows
As well because
You are alone
I can't explain this but
I smile and this is all
I can say for today

Perhaps it's a kind of revenge
For these few years
I decided to forget
About myself
And about few true wishes I had
And about you
When I decided to be
Happy married woman and mother too
To the man I thought
Can be this better one
Than you were, my Love
But I came back
To my dreams about you
And now you are inside
As my man again
I don't know
What should I do
But one is sure
I still love you
And this feeling
Keeps me alive

Because everything around
Is too boring and too hard
To enjoy all these
Lovely whiles and things
Of real life
You came back to my dreams
And I feel great
With you within
Because only you
Are this man
Who could realized my dreams
About something special
Something different, new
Of something I would
Taste all my life through
You are my dream
You are my knight
And nothing can change
This fact that
I'm again alive
Having you inside.

Touch of love

The fresh tender
Touch of love
I felt suddenly
This morning
In the fisherman glance
Which hypnotized me
By his wonderful
Blue eyes as I saw once
And which seems to be
So familiar to me
I can't stop think about this
I know we will never
Probably have a opportunity to
Meet each other more deeply but
I'll go tomorrow there
To buy the fish from this man
To have a chance just to look
At his wonderful eyes again
I know I could fall in love with him
I did this somehow
In this simply tender way
Which doesn't expect
Any beginning and any end
It's just a while which invades me
Rapes my thoughts
And I'm again
In influence of
Some stranger
Love scent touch
When I feel this sweet tendrils
Around my soul
And I know
That this is one of these men
Who could be
Some special one to me
If we could meet
In a different time
And different way
Than today.

Every kind of love

I think that this what I like the most
Is this scent of love I feel in the air
When I see such eyes as today
Then I can imagine myself
With this man who I find so special
And in some way who can be mine
Mostly this is the beginning and the end of the story
Between me and such a man as I saw this morning
I like imagine about the life of this man
Who seems to be so charming guy
With this "something" in his eye
Yesterday I saw the car too
With the license plate
I found from your land is
And it was so exciting, when
I imagined that it's you who came
To me suddenly then
I know it's a little funny
To imagine such things
And live by this
But it's something what I like
Maybe even more
Then a good dinner
In a fancy restaurant
Even more than the evening
With my husband and child
I'm looking for the touch of love
In the eyes and voice
Of the man I can meet on my way
My husband looked so familiar too
I saw in him the father
Maybe it's the reason we
Are together
But you
You were always
Just a man
The man and lover
And you stayed like that
Inside
You are the man I love
And I wish to be forever with
In dreams or in reality
However

Waiting, making love, touching
Feeling, being above

Every different kind of love
Is the reason I live in this world.

I wish to go a Paris with you

How it would be nice
To go to Paris
Just for a week,
or month or more
I don't know how long, my Love
We will feel wonderful there
Together
I can imagine
This lovely little room
The dressing-table for me
And this grand bed
For young lovers as we are still
We could spend a lot of time
There and then
In the morning we will get
Some croissants
With the chocolate hot
And then
Make love again
So soft and so sweet
And after some time
We could go to the city
To see some lovely things in

To walk on the streets
To go to a restaurant
For a dinner in a French style
And speak about something nice
About some little signs
About pretty day and the night
About this how wonderful time we spent
Together
And then in the evening
We could dance
Within one of the fancy club
For salsa, tango or something like that
And then go to bed
Again
And after that
Maybe we could visit
Some gallery too

Louvre for example
To see all these beauty sights
From dreams of old artists
To feel the spirit of ancient days
And to try to imagine
My self in all these lives
In all these faces
Innocence age

I wish I wish
All these little clouds
Of feelings when you are in love
In the city which seems to be
A paradise for lovers
As you and me

I wish I wish to make love
In the night
Down the bridge
In the ships lights
And the sounds of life
Around

I wish I wish to spend
Some time
In the city like this
With my lover
And dance on the street
With this melody from my dreams
As a gypsy girl
I wish to be sometimes.

Date on the boat

There is a lot of fishermen around
But I see only this one
He was absent for a few days
And I felt a kind of lonely space
Here on this beach
Full of people around
Who don't exist to me at all
I was looking for his boat
And I knew that
I will see him again
So I was waiting

Today I feel
That you will be by the sea
Yes you are there
I can't stop smiling seeing your face
And I know that you are looking at me
The same way when I'm going
And I know that you want I'd come to you
Just to smile or speak

So I should do something
I think

I see you just sit waiting
Smiling, so I stopped and asked
"Did you catch something
Interesting today?"
"Yes", you said
"A very big fish I got".
We start to speak
And I don't know
How it happened but I asked:
"Do you need some help
Because I'd like to try
To see how it is
Fishing in the sea"
And you said:" yes
I can take you with me
But not tomorrow yet
Because tomorrow I can't
But how long you will stay here?
Yes I'd like to take you with me

To the sea"

So we have a date on the boat
I think it is something special
How it's nice
I was scared to ask
I was afraid to start
But I knew he was waiting for me
His eyes and smile was telling me
Come on girl
It's you who are beautiful
On this beach
It's you who I'm looking for
I couldn't stop this smile too
I love this feeling
It's coming so rarely
When I'm in love
At the first sight
I'm not sure who has chosen who
By his look
I remember now these eyes blue
And I know he is smiling this way just to me
Because he see the beautiful woman in me
It's very courageous to start to speak
With him first

So, I smile today
My fisherman came back
And I'll probably meet him
Better soon
Because I feel he wants this
And I want this too.

I saw him again on the beach
I feel his presence stronger
Than everything and
It makes the smile on my face
I make decisions in my mind all the time
Where he is there where I am
I'm thinking about this
How to start conversation with him
Because he is always at work
Near his boat and he never try
To come to me as I see
He is just looking by his eyes
For me and smile

So, today I came closer again
To this man

And I asked of this trip that we have planned
But unfortunately he had some accident today
with the engine
So I must wait few days
To take a ride with him on his boat
But it's strange that after conversation
I'm not so much with him as I was before
The feelings changed
It's a little bit sad
Or maybe not

It's just how feelings come and go

The nature of this is still a kind of miracle.

I have to go

The true problem is
That I always knew
Who I wanted to live with
But I wasn't strong enough
To show to him
How I feel
But I live in this hope
For him again
Because he didn't say no
As I asked
And this is enough to me
To live inside this dream.

I'm sorry my lovely husband
But I can't cry all my life
That I didn't chose a right guy
I need to try to be sure
That it can be a real love
I know what I feel
But I don't know his soul
After years

But I need to try
To speak with him again
I know he doesn't want
To break this what I have
But I know that I want him
More than everything in this world
I'm sorry then but I must go.

No choice I have

So, you are not there
Where you should be
I'm afraid it kind of trick can be
Or maybe you really had to go abroad
I don't know
As always you are gone
When I'm ready to go
To you, my Love
As always
You live in my dreams
Only
I don't have anything so far
Any sign to be sure of your heart
I started to write some messages again
But I know you don't get it at all
You know it is a little sad
That you are only in my mind
Always
But I couldn't stop writing
Every day I have
Something to say to you
That I'm OK
That I see you everywhere
That's all right
That's good
Even this silence of yours
That I can look
Positive at this fact
That you are still absent
In my life
Untaken messages
Every day
I don't know why
I still believe
In some signs
That it can be love
Am I wrong
Who knows?
Who can tell me
If not you?
I must wait
I don't have
Any choice
Because I love
You.

Hamburger

There is nothing more stressful to me in this world
Than eating the hamburger on the train station bar
So far
It's so big with so many things inside
And this is just not possible
To open your mouth so wide
To eat this without panic in your heart
That you can't get it right
And everything will go down
On the ground or on the table around
I did this maybe three times
I mean I bought it
And its always this same
I can't eat this hamburger
Not because of its taste
Which is quite normal bread vegetable meat and sauce
But because of this stress
I need to fight with a piece of bread
And I do but after that
I promise myself
Never again!
How people do this
How they can eat
Such difficult things
Maybe they have better tooth
I don't know
Recently I was smarter than before
I got some fork but
It doesn't help too much
It's always very hard
So it was the last time
I bought the hamburger
I swear.

Are you afraid I'm not serious?

You know who I am
You know what I want
So, come baby
Come on
Let's do it
What's wrong?
What are you afraid about?
Don't you wish to be my man again?
Don't you want to be my toy
To play with at all?
Maybe you are afraid

That I'd be bored
After a while
And that I could throw you out?

So be with me
As a man interesting enough
To stay longer with
Be the man I know
You were to me
And I think
I'll lose control
As I want
Because so far
I can't find
Another man
Who has enough power
To take me all
With my heart and soul
As I need
As I want
My master
Come on
Come to me
I'm waiting
For you still
In my dreams.

Life

Life is just a collection
Of the different
Impressions which exists
During a day
Inside us and around
This place we live in
It's kind of mish-mash
Of our feelings
Thoughts and this is
What really happens
To us
During these lessons
We get all the time
In our life.

I know you are good man

I like this what you wrote to me
Recently
It helps me to believe
That you are a special man to me
I know you are not so bad
As I said to you
I know you care
I know you try to understand
I know you are a good man
And I still feel warm in my heart to you
But I'm afraid
This marriage can't be good
For both of us
For me and you too
There is something inside me
What makes me still think
About another life
About another place
Beside him
And I know that it hurts you
But there is nothing I can do for it
I'm still the woman who lives
By my dream
And I can't just throw out him
From my heart
I couldn't live without him
I couldn't work, I couldn't smile
Without his sight inside my mind
You are still so handsome one
And you know
What is right and what is wrong
I respect your mind but
Sometimes I think
That I'm not so good as you are
I like to be a little rude one
And this how you think
I should live I just can't
I love my fantasies
I love to be as I am inside
Without too many rules sometimes
I feel free then
And more happy
So, I think we can't be together
If you can't understand
Even this that
I need him so much

I need my lover to feel alive
I need my lover to smile
But if I'll go I hope
That you will forgive me
That I didn't love you
Strong enough to stay forever
I hope you can understand
You are the smart man
I know I should hide this
I know you shouldn't know
To save this marriage
But I can't be silent
When I love
I know it hurts you
And it hurts you strong
But this that you couldn't
Forgive me
Is the reason I should go
If you can't live with me and him
You must live alone
Because he is my soul
Without this man I couldn't live anymore
I always loved him and I always will
Even if he doesn't want me
Right now and right here
He lives inside me
And he will stay there forever
I tried to forget him
But I wasn't complete
I wasn't myself to the end
Now I know this
And I can live with this
But you don't
Even if everything happens
Only in my mind
It's too hard for you
So, I can't
I can't live with you
Because I'm cheating on you
All the time even sleeping in your arms
I know it is sad for you
I know it hurts but
He is the man I love most
And I can't pretend anymore
That I'm only yours
Because it is not truth.

Dear Love

Just be enough to me
And please
If you'd ever need
Someone like me
If you ever feel lonely,
Sick, depressed, fail, or just not OK
Call me and
I'll come, always
Please don't forget my name
Don't forget my address
And I'll come, always
Even if I should go to the end of the world
I'll come
Not because I'm sad for you
But because I love you
And perhaps
It could be the only chance to me
To stay by your side for a while
Please don't be so proud
Just don't forget and call
If You ever need me, please
If I said or did
Something stupid, forgive me
I didn't mean anything wrong
You are this man I never forget
In my heart and I hope that
We will have a chance to meet
Someday
If it be your will
I'm here

Always love

Anna

Going to you

I'm going
I can't believe
I'm going to him
I couldn't wait
Another year
I couldn't wait another ten
I'm going
To see him
Nervous?
No, I'm not
Nervous
A little calm but
I'm just going
To see my Love
I'm going to know
I'm going to finish
Or start
I'm going
To take apart
I'm going to you
That's all
I'm going
To see my Love
I'm going but
What I'll tell you
After ten years?
What I'll tell you
After this year?
What I'll tell you
Do I have some thoughts yet?
What I'll tell you?
I don't know yet
But I'm going
I'm going to see my Love
To see your face
To see your eyes
To see your smile
I'm going
Because I can't stop
I can't stop what?
I can't stop thinking about you
Is it not enough?
I feel a little empty now
I don't know
Do I say any word to you
I'm a little scared but

I'm going
It's just what I have to do
To finish this play with you

This is the end

This is the end
The end of this
Story of love
Which has never existed
Anywhere just
In memory in thoughts
Just in my mind
Just in dreams I have had
I'm sorry but
This is really the end
I don't have
Anything to say
To you
Just that
The real life
Is never like
You dream about
But, by the way
I don't regret
Any word
Any poem
Any dream I have had
You are a part
Of me somehow
Just a little part of me now
And you will stay
As a memory
Of this perfect love
I have never had before
It's nobody fault
It's just a life
No, I'm not unhappy
No, but
I just know
What I wanted to know
And now I'm calm
I can live somehow
Just like that
It doesn't hurt me
Yes I have
A few tears
The tears which are

Just a regret
That real life
Is never the same
As we dream about
And that
This love is gone
Just like that
No hope anymore
No light
It's gone with the wind
Somehow
Do you know
It's just a life
That's all
You could be my man
But we lost this chance
Many years ago
So, it's gone
So, what to do now?
Do you know?
Live, I suppose
Just live and smile again
Free from love
Incredible
But I loved you the most
I can't say I don't
But I understand
That you don't
So, everything is clear now
Good bye, my Love
Good bye.

Be realistic you said

Be realistic and don't live by the past
You said and this is all I wanted to know
To be sure that I was just an episode to you
That's all
No, you are not bad
No, you just live
Your own world today
But don't say that
You don't know me now
Because you should know
I'm just as I am
And as I was before
And everything is here
You can come and see
And it was in my eyes before
You were just silent too long
To not let grow
All these dreams, all these words
Which were born in the past
And flowed away from my heart today
Now I'm just free from this love
I kept so long within my soul
I'm free from you, mon amour
To live in reality again
Without this ghost that you were
My sweet English boy I've met once
You stay like that to me
Just in my dreams
So, don't worry
I wont let you know again
That I'd like to see you
In reality, my old friend
You are the most romantic love
I have ever had
So, thank you for that you were
My man
Maybe in next life
We will meet again?
But in this life we can't
I know, I understand
It's not possible to move the rock
If you couldn't help
If you don't want this same

But I know that you are right
My man
I know I must stop this love
So I did, believe me
I understand everything
Just don't say
You don't know me
Because I think you know a lot
I was never more open
As right now
During this year through
When you could read me
As an open book
I did everything you could know me, I thought
But if you don't
So, I was wrong
Your side of this story was quite short
You know?
But If you could love me
This way I loved you
We could change the world
We could be so happy
As no one was never before
I suppose but...
Life is just a life
And love is just love
As everybody knows.

Can I come back?

I set free my heart
From the ghost of love
I had within my soul
And now I'm back
I can try to love again
The real man as you are
The husband of mine
Would you try?
Or is it too late for us?
Tell me because
I know now
Much more than before
And you too, my love
So, we can try again
Yes we can
Just don't crash this
By stupid thoughts
and silence anymore
Let's be again
Together
As never before
Would you like
To come home?
I'm here again
A little changed
I know it was hard to you
I know I hurt you but
I'm still your wife
And the mother of
These children we have
So, let's try again
My real man
What do you think?
It'd work
To live happily together?
After this while of the war
Within my soul that ended
Just a second ago
Please let's try
It's still worth I hope
Yes let's try
To fight for this love, for us
Not only for the children we have
Do you believe me?
That it could work?
Let's try again my Love.

Just one thing

But this what
I can't be sure of
Is this if your words to me
All these words you said
It's because
You don't love me
And never loved or because
I'm mother and wife
And it's just too hard for you now
I don't know but
You couldn't love me too much
If you never tried
To show me yourself
After some time
Yes you are right
This what I know so far
Is just you from these few days
We had very long time ago
What I was just
Keeping in my heart
But you are right
It's not enough to be sure
Of anything at all
But you know
It was just this touch of love
Too strong to me I suppose
And this works in a special way
That I just feel you and I know
Everything about you
I don't need your words then
To understand
Who you are
What you want
And what you don't
I can't explain this but
It works somehow
So, I know now everything
What I wanted

Just a while is enough to know
The man you love
I've never felt someone
So much as you
But I know also
That you don't feel the same
So, this is the end

Yes this is the end
I just need to explain to my self
This fact and everything
Is going to be all right
All right

Just one thing

To let me live in peace, please
Tell me that you never loved me
That you have never planned
To be with me seriously
That your call phone after
These three years
It was just like that
Like a call phone to a friend
That you haven't done
Your Polish business
Thinking that it could be
Just a possibility for us
That you have never had
Me in your plans for a happy life
And that you didn't come back
To Poland now thinking about
This little while in the past
And that maybe you could find me again
Of course with the hope in your heart that
I'm alone right now, no?

So, it's fine
I'm not going to move
From my town yet
If you could say this
That I was just a dreamer
And that you have never thought
Of me through all these years
And then I'll be OK
Just say it!
As you said that
I should be more responsible right now
And that you are living in South
And I'm living in North
And this is also a problem as well like this
That you like travel to live
But you know that I like this too
And travels is this what I lack in my life, so
It is not so important at this case so much
Important is that I must resign from you

Because you want this, that's all
And I know it's only a way
To stop this dream completely
Before I'll really go

Be responsible, be responsible
I remember, I know
Be happy
I'm happy, but because?
Because of these words
And this hope for a great love
So, let's find another reason to smile
Freedom from your sight in my mind
For example?

Just the last thing I need
Just tell me this please
I'm not crazy woman as you see
We can speak normally, I think
So, just tell me this one thing
That you never really loved me
And you will be free completely from me.

Yes you have been changed
A little but not too much
You are still full of charm
Of course you tried
To explain that you are not the same
That you are living now a different way
No I don't think so
And all I can see now
All what has been changed
It's just that you wanted me
And now you don't
This is the change what I feel the most
But I understand your coldness
I can understand
Your escape to the real world
Yes, you are strong man
As you have always been
But this is also what I loved in you
My man
The man who not exist for me anymore
It is sad to realised
This fact after years, you know?
Just a bit sad
But it is my fault
Because I couldn't
I just couldn't stop

Dream of you
My Love
But I'll do this now
Yes I'll do, I'll try
Because now I'm sure
I'm sure that you don't want me at all
So live and try to be happy
As you wish
And I'll be happy too
Yes this is something I can do
Not because of you
Not for you
For my self, I suppose
And for few person yet
Who live very close to me
Yes I'll try, I think
To be happy in my way but
I understand too
That you are not
Interested of this too much
So, maybe I'll write
To somebody else
As I did to you
Because this is something
I love to do
Yes, write and love and feel again the man
Who loves me too
This is my way to be happy, I know
And try again something new
This is wonderful
I hope you know this too
I hope all your dreams come true
What ever it is my love.

I don't know you
You think
Of course
I don't know your new dreams
I don't know your borders too
Even your plans but
I know you, I think
I know you and I will
But it was sad to me
To hear that
You don't know me still
I thought that showing you my soul
Is enough that you could
Know me and trust

But you were closed
Yes you were closed
You want to be
A kind of stranger to me
But you can't be like that
I'm sorry
But make love to you
Wont be good I think
Yes wont be good
You didn't want this
I felt you didn't want me
No, it doesn't hurt me too much
It's just a fact
And I can understand you
If you want to know
I had this same feeling before
To someone else some time ago
Yes, I think that I know
But of course I regret
That we couldn't even
Stay friends
I just felt
You don't want me anymore
And that you were scared
This situation and
You don't see any future for you and me
Yes that's all I felt from you
So, when you hugged me
I thought that
It wasn't necessary
I didn't feel your warm
I didn't need this at all
Yes it was quite too long
And now I understand everything so clear
But don't tell me
That's all because I'm unhappy
It's not like that
No, I can't agree
With such a bly bly
Don't tell me that living by my past
Is not right, yes you are the man
Who I've met a very long time ago
But it wasn't just a past
What was keeping me
by your side through this year
It was the memory,
Dreams and a new hopes too
For you with me

But you didn't get this
As something good for you
So, I understand, I understand you
I suppose
It's pretty clear to me
I should stop to think this way about you
That's all that's all that's all I can do
After this meeting with you
And I know too
That you are not able to risk anything
For love, perhaps because
You are not in love
And you have your different pretty world
To live by, yes it's clear
But I just have hope
That someday you will find her
This right girl to you
Who makes you believe
That love is important too to live
Even this not right to the end
Not responsible, not married
Yes I wish you that you could believe
That not everything depends from you only
Especially happiness which lives inside you
I wish you love, because everything else you have
And you can realize by yourself
My independent man
I hope that you could just understand me
And this crazy year
I have been living through
With all these memories and dreams of you
And that you could
Stop to be so confused
Because of this fact
And try to enjoy that
There was some woman in love
So crazy for you so long
And that she was ready to risk
Everything she have had
Just to check how it could be
Living together with you, my sweet
Yes, I really have hope
That you could just enjoy this
Because all of this I've done
It was just to pleased you, my love
But if you don't want this love
You know you are free
And I can still live

And smile too, my friend
Yes I still think about you this way
And you always will be
Someone very special to me
I hope you like this
Even if we never meet
Don't forget that I'm a little poet
And I love to be in love
And to give my love in words, in smile
In dreams however I can
So, just realize this fact
And smile when you think about me
Please just be the friend of mine
In your mind
That's all I wish now and I care of
From the special man as you are
And never be confused
This what I write to you or not to you
Just be my muse from time to time
And I'll be fine and full of joy
To every boy and girl in this world
Smile, smile my friend
And be happy, be free again
That's my wish, you should respect this
If you just like me a little still.

Yes, you have a little right too
You are not a romantic man anymore
You couldn't do anything to make me feel
A bit more comfortable with you my dear
This short conversation behind the door
No, it wasn't nice at all
You are right you are not this same man
As you were some time ago
But it's just maybe because you don't want me
or maybe not, I don't know
What were happened with you, my Love
You can't fly anymore, not at all
It's terrible, you are like a boy
In this way you tread the woman too
You just don't know what to do
With your lady, hey it's sad, my Love
You should change something with this, I suppose
But maybe it's just to me, you are so mean
I hope you didn't turn over a new leaf so completely

Oh it can't be, such a wonderful boy

Became so coarse, and he is just a nice but so formal and prim
but not real just closed and scared, I don't understand
What were happened with you, my friend
You shouldn't be like that
No, you couldn't be with me being like this
No, it wasn't in a good style, I think
But I hope it was just because you didn't know that I'll come
And that you were just a little scared by the way and busy too
But you know, sometimes you shouldn't do things
Like this, but on the other hand it was great way to leave
If it was the reason, then I can understand but
I think that something miss in you somehow
Just think about this little suggestion,
For a better future with love in your life and heart
Just tread the woman as a lady not as a little child
Please, please I think it wasn't nice
No, it wasn't a nice "good bye"
You should just try to be as a man again
Not only as traveller or a businessman
Do you really know what is so good for you?
I'm not sure, my Love, I'm not sure
But yes I perfectly understand
That I'm no one to you, my friend
I was ready to risk everything
Which wasn't so bad, I think
To show how important, how real you were
And you are not ready to do anything
Yes you just let me see that I mean nothing
but don't worry I'm all right
I just needed to know
How it is with you right now
And I think it wasn't worth to risk
Yes you have your charm still but
It's just because I see you as the man I loved
But I feel right now that you are not worth of this love
Because you can't get and offer anything at all
You are like a rock, hard boy with a lot of joy within
So, Good bye, Good bye
You are not worth any change in my life
Even having your sweet eyes
But something happened with your smile with your warm inside
No, I don't love this man you are right now
But it's good, it's just this what you wanted
So, everything is all right
And you know what I think after a while?
That perhaps you could be good to me
but to bed only to nothing more
Yes you are still too attractive this way

But this is not too much for a long distance relationship
And besides if you don't want me
It is still without any sense – Yes
I think it wont be very difficult to forget you now
You are much smaller than you were before
And you know why?
Because I have done this
It's me who made you so great
but now I see you in different way just as a normal man
Yes I feel a lot yet and I suppose
It could be nice just to sleep with you but
No, you are not this man you were before
You couldn't understand me at all
No, you are not this same man to me
So, maybe it's good time
To leave
Yes, you have showed me
That you live in my past only
And it's OK, maybe you wanted this
Maybe you even don't know
But everything is changed from now
You are like any other man
You are not so perfect
Yes, the charm splashed
Perhaps I could even hate you after some time

So, maybe it's great that we never even start
Maybe I can be as a whore
I was ready to leave my husband for old love
But you are nothing to me at all
Because you can't love anymore
And only this is really important to me
As you maybe know
So, good by, my Love

Hey but smile, it's just thoughts
Just feelings I had for a while which
Flowed from my heart but
I don't think so bad about you now
I just try to let my soul say everything
What was growing in my head so far
After this short while with you I have had

Mix of emotions

The strange feelings I have for you
Some are as a little child
So shameful, innocent and fine
Some are as a woman who is watching
Your every move,
Every single part of your body through
Just tasting inside your charm
And there is another one
Feeling in my looking for you
From the distance too
I see everything what you haven't done
More critical I am
And this what is missing in the way you stick with me
My love, I see you now, so differently
I'm a little confused over these feelings I have
Some are changed, some are dead
Sometimes again, so fresh yet
Sometimes I'm so cruel and so bad too
No, you are not a past yet
But soon you will be, don't worry
I'm working on this
Very hard as you see.

Just live a while

You were not worth these words I had to you
But I play well with this so you can do it too
If you wish but if you don't... well...
Stop reading me, only you know and I
Who I'm writing to this part of my life but
Don't forget it's just a write not reality
So, you don't have to be so confused, I think
You know how reality looks like now
There is almost nothing between us
You are afraid to be close to me
I was scared to be this woman I wish to be
So, there is no way to be together, I think
No, maybe as a dream, you can still be with me
But no one more
Yes, do you understand now
Who you really are to me?
Inspiration, I think
Just inspiration to live
I need the passion within my heart
To be happy, to smile
But passion in reality doesn't exist, I see
So, let's dream, let's love again
Whoever we want, because here
We can be so free as we want to be
This is all the joy of life
I feel inside,
All these whiles to catch
But how long?
Who knows, it's not important
Live the whiles that's all
You are married or you are alone
Just catch the whiles and live
As you can and as you want
This is a wish for you and me too
I know that you have
The similar philosophy, I see
Just to be happy
I'm happy like that
And please never think that
I'd try to force you to my side
If you don't want this, if you don't see us
I'm the free spirit, my Love
I have the family too but it is not a point
And don't think that I don't remember about them
Yes I know and I try to do everything good
But you see more problems than me

That's all I think is against this love
And of course this that you don't love me at all
But how come you tell that you don't know me now
I've started to write in your language
That you could understand me
That you could read me as an open book I am to you
The most real me, as I ever can be
That you could know all my life, whole me
All my dreams, desires, wishes, sins
And you say that you don't know me
Reading me from a year
The whole story of my life and love
Where you took the first place within
But you still don't know me then, OK,
I think I understand you don't want me
Yes it's not a point that you don't know
But this that you are scared this what I showed
Who I am and who I could be
For you here.

You were as you should be

I needed this to know
What is going on
In the real situation
And now I'm just calm
I think you were great
You were just as you should be
Cold and stiff but it's good for me
To try to forget
To lose all illusions I have had
And to come back to real life again
So, thank you, my friend
You are a very special man
But I understand
We can't change the past
Anyway
It was good to see you again.

The most I love to be in love

Today I think of you
In a different way again
I love this distance and the time between us
This long time when we don't see each other
I'm happy and I think you did right
Every word you said
But I said something, you know
Something what is not true
To the end
That I'm not happy
With my husband
And you know I feel relief
After all these words you said
That I should be responsible
For children I have
That I should try again
To fight for this love
And to fix my marriage
And about this that I should be a realist
You were right
Just one thing I didn't like
When you said that I have to look
The way to be happy and not to live by the past
Because I think I'm happy now
Living in the past, the present and in the future too
I love every dimensions of my life
And this memory of you
I think I love it the most but
I know now that there is no way to be together
I'm glad to understand this
But did you say goodbye to me too?
I didn't hear you clear I think
And something else
What you said about this that
I could find a way to be happy and to know
What I want in my life
I think I know this
You didn't realize yet?
I love to write
I love to be the observer of the life
I love to catch the whiles
I love to be a shining star sometimes
But the most, the most
I love to be in love
I love to feel love in the air, so
I think I know what is good to me

I think it was the best choice I did
I mean husband and children I have but
I still have you in me yet
And this what I have done last year
This that I told you everything
Was something I needed to do to be sure
To give to us the last chance
For whatever we will want and choose
But you know, I feel relief now
That you realized me
That there is no way to us to you and me
Outside this dream
I needed to hear these words
To live in peace and to love in real
My husband, my children
My family too
And all this world around
With you too
But free from this what I had to do.

Thank you to let me dream

I wish to thank you again
That you let me live in this dream
So long, so deeply
This is something I appreciate now
After a while when I lost all illusions but
I'm free and I can try again
To love this way as I know I can
Someday
Not you, my love but
This is not a point, you know
I'll love this one who will need and want
This one who could be as I wish
Who could compare all these dreams
This someone special because
It's not easy at all
To give your heart to everyone
It's just doesn't work
Doesn't sing at all
I don't know when I'll feel
So much love in my heart again
To sing, to dance, to fly
As I did with you somehow
But I hope that someday
I'll love again this way
This hope I'll live from today.

I loved you but

I loved you
Because I thought
You loved me too
When I knew you didn't
I stopped
It wasn't difficult at all
I just know
You don't need me
So, I must go
This is not a way
I should go
That's all
Yes I feel a little
Empty now
But someday
I'll feel this way as with you again
So, you don't need to be afraid of me now
I can survive everything
Even this simple real life, I think.

You were cold enough

Yes you did everything well
You were cold enough
To let me believe
That you don't love me
And that I should
Forget and finish this case
Ten years, ten years and a half
When I had this love and
A little hope for us somehow
And now I know that it's over
I don't need to care for you
I don't need to be so unsure
Looking for another man
That you could come back
It's over now
And I think I'm OK
I just need to love again
Love somebody else, but how?
How to do it right now?
I don't know yet
But I believe
It's not the end
Of the world
To lose the one you loved.

Be a realist

I hate this word
I hate and why I must
Hear this so many times
"Be a realist"
I hate to be a realist
Why should I like this, why
I hate to be just a good wife
I hate to live in my town all my life
I need to fly
I hate this science carrier too
I want to be an artist, a poet, a writer, a dancer too
Whatever it's not important at all
I want to be a woman in love
But I don't need to be a realist
No, no, no
I hate this kind of job
Be a realist means to me
Just live normally but it is so
Boring and mean
It's like nothing just things without any meanings
I never want to be a realist no
And I wish to find someone
Who lets me not be a realist
Who lets me fly who, lets me sing
I need love to dream about
I need the touch, so shy

I need the whole world in my hand
I want real love to start again
And new dreams about the perfect man
Who is touching me by his soul
So wild, so proud, so deep and so warm
By his merrily flowing thoughts and palms
I wish to be real but not a realist at all
Every age, every time is great
To feel so good to feel OK
With this sensual dance
Living in an imaginary embrace
Of my thoughts, so hungry
This voice, this touch, this caress
This deep ocean of desires
Hidden somewhere in the cave of their eyes
And within mine and your soul
Still so mysterious, so unknown.

I didn't want anything wrong

Who said that you are bad?
It's not like that my honey boy
I just tried to show you
Myself after years
That you could decide
That you could have the choice
But of course if you don't want
It doesn't have any sense
It's nobody's fault, my love
Everything is OK
I'm just free from you
And now I just need
To find my own way
Or someone so great to love again
With such a strength
But believe me it's not so easy
You were too good or you just came
At this right moment
I don't know now how it was but
It's you who were so important to me
All this time, through all these years
But perhaps you were right
I'm too difficult sometimes
And living with me could be sometimes hard
Besides you have different plans
And I have two children and of course
It would be a problem for us
For you and for them too
Yes, you did well it's just too late
I understand

I think that all I need is just a light
To see the passion inside
To write, to smile, to live
And to be free, from all persons I can't live with
From all this simple tiring things
From all these thoughts that I'm not good enough
To survive in this difficult world
Where sometimes it's so hard to satisfy everyone
And not forget about yourself
And about this wishes you need to realise
But you know when I was going to you
I was ready for everything
Of course I had a little hope too
That you will come to the train station

And that you take me to your home
But of course I didn't count on this too much
So it wasn't so bad that you were absent again
I was just angry and sad
After these few hours when I had to wait
And then your secretary said
That possibly you wont come today
I came to you just to know how it is with you
I didn't want to say or do anything wrong
And against you and I thought
That you are just hiding yourself
And it wasn't nice to me no, it wasn't nice at all,
But you came at the end so now it's OK
I just know what to think and what to do
It was very important and necessary meeting to me
So, thank you that you were there at the end
Even so busy as always but it's OK
I just know what I wanted to know
So I didn't waste any hour.

Happy dreamer

I'm just happy again with myself
I just need to be careful
To not say too much
About my future plans
Because I don't want another war today
So, I'm living in silence
But it's OK
I know that I just need
To wait for this right time
With this right place
Children please grow up
That they could stop
Telling me what should I do
With my life to
Please grow up to your mother
That she could get the world
That she could fly
And go wherever she wants
With you of course
I wish to live in London
In New York and Paris
I wish to find something
Interesting to me, some job, some people
New air, something completely new, I guess
I'm a little tired of this place
It's just a dream I have
But soon I'll go
And I'll find a way
I'll find a home again
And I'll love and hate
But I'll live
I'll live as no one else.

Real life is never the same

Your philosophy of life
Is quite easy to understand
We all want to be just happy
So, me too and this what I did
This that I opened my heart to you
Was just great to me to feel like that
But now I'm just not sure
If it was good to you too
If you were just confused
So, I'm sorry to take your time, my Love
I hope you will be all right soon
I just wanted to give to us this last chance
For a little romance
Writing this love story I set free my heart
So, again thank you for that you let me be
As I wish sometimes - so completely free
In this what I want and feel
You let me be real and you let me to dream
And I think that I love this the most
More than live because real life is never
So pretty and fine as this one in your heart and mind.

The sense of my life

Living in my little place of this world
That I know quite well
Is this what I want to leave
Someday
And this is my point of view
Of my own reality too
I wish to escape
From this world
That's all

Enjoying this tour
Of my own escape
From everything I have
And I know so well

Escape to the world
Still so big, so mysterious, so unknown
Which is waiting for me
That I'll come
To make it smiling and to hold
Some small parts of it

How I wish to go
To the huge world
To capture all of its miracles
To meet new people too
Looking for love

Looking for wisdom flowing from their souls
To capture all these songs of life
From every town, every city, I could find
From every heart

To know more about this life
To know more about myself
It's the sense of my life I suppose
To leave this town, to know more
About whole this world and me

And this joy of leaving something
I love escapes, I think
And I love to live here
Because I can go away someday.

Do your thing

Do your thing
What do you mean?
Do you think it is so easy
To build your own life
As you wish
And to be happy inside still

Do your thing
What, what it can be
Do you really believe
In your words?

Do your thing
All right then
I'll love
Because I love this
The most and then
I will work around myself
And around this love I have
Doing my things
To enjoy this
Yes it's quite easy to say
Just hard to believe.

About all these things that make us happy or sad

What are these things that make you happy?
There are a lot of them
It's when you have
Someone to hug
It's when you have
Someone to care about
It's when you have
Someone to love
It's when you have
Someone to lose
It's when you have
Someone to talk to
It's when you have some money too
It's when you bought
Something nice and new
It's when you have
Something to dream about
It's when your work is fine
It's when someone is looking at you
This way you love to
It's when you feel still pretty and young
It's when your heart is open for the new one
It's when you are not afraid to be yourself
It's when people around are so nice and they like you
It's when you have something to do
It's when you do something nice to someone
Or when you do something not right too
It's depends sometimes, you know
It's when someone loves you too
It's when you just live and smile
It's when you know something
It's when you are not sad or depressed

Then you are not happy too much
At times when you lack something
What you still don't have but you are looking for
It's when someone say or do
What is not nice to you
And when you just can't feel so great
To be happy a whole day
It's when you don't believe in yourself
That you are good enough to do something
Special in this world
It's when you are afraid

To do something with your life
What maybe you have to do, sometimes
It's hard to know all these things
That make you feel
Happy one or not too much
There is a lot of things as you know

Am I happy with my marriage?
I don't know
Sometimes yes, sometimes no
I don't regret I have
This life but
Sometimes I wish to try again
With someone else
Or just dream about this
It's hard to say but
No I'm not unhappy, no
Then I know a little more than before
When I finish some part of my life again
And I can go somewhere I don't know where yet

I like to be a little unsure
Of my future too, I think
I don't like to know everything
So, am I happy or not?
Yes I think I'm quite a happy person
Just sometimes, no
When someone is not as I want
Or when someone can't understand
This is what I try to explain
When I have too much on my mind or too little
Or when I'm a bit lost inside
But these are just a whiles so
I don't need to worry about it
Too much and live again with the smile
Because I can, I can do a lot yet
And I know what is the most important too
It's love, love in your heart
Love to one person or to not only one
Just love, love in your mind
To whole the world sometimes

I was unhappy for a while
Because I didn't know
What do you think about

And what do you want
And now I know and now
I'm calm and happy again
Without this fear
That there is something wrong in the air
I didn't want to be a fool all the time
I needed to know
What is real at this story of love
I had and I was within
I don't like
This kind of silence
For too long
So, that's why
I came
And I don't regret
I know more than before
That's all
And I hope you stopped to
Look at me
As for someone crazy
And to whom
It is not possible to speak.

I was just lost in my mind

No, my Love I'm happy
With my marriage and life
I was just lost in my mind
After this phone call when
I heard your voice again
And I was lost in feelings
I couldn't stop thinking of the past
About everything
I just don't know
Why you left me
To live this way so long
Why you didn't stop me before
I started all this show
I don't know if it was worth it
I don't think so but perhaps
There is the time yet to repair
Everything between me and the husband I have
I hope he can forgive me and understand
But it wont be easy to him to live with me, with this
He can't be so sure of me anymore
And this love
I think I destroyed something but
I needed to show you
One more time
That I can, I can do everything
For you
But I was wrong

Strange human nature
I was dying from love for you
One year through
And now when I know
That you don't love me
I'm happy again
To be free

Don't you understand
That all I've done
It was for you?
But you didn't even get
Anything from this

I almost destroyed my world
Just to show you
That I care and love
To give you this chance

To be my man again and you
Didn't even have a courage
To say no
I don't want this, silly man
Don't you understand
That I was real to you?
I was ready to do
Everything what I said
Why you didn't stop me
I can't understand
I'm sorry but
This what you said recently
You could do a one year ago
And I wouldn't be so fool so long

I'm happy person, mostly
If you don't know
I was just sad because of you
Because of your silence too
Because I didn't know
What you felt for me
And I was sad
That I'm not the single one
To be with you
If you would love me too
But if you don't
It's just the end
And it's great
Don't you understand?
If you can't speak with me
You are right I don't know you
I don't understand
What do you want to get
By your stupid silence
I didn't like
How you were to me so, I think
I don't need to see you anymore
It wasn't nice at all
So, you have nothing
And I have much more
I have open heart and love
And my world is much more real than yours
You are just a nice guy that's all
You are not this man for me anymore
After this what you have done
By your silence by this hiding
By last meeting when I had to wait

Too long for you
I think that you are rude!
So, good bye again
I'm so happy to say it, yes I am
I can't believe I was so stupid
To try to leave everything I love
Only because this memory
I had within my soul
Stupid man, why you didn't say
That you just don't want this
before
Why you couldn't come to meet me and say
This what I was asking for?
Didn't you realize that
It wasn't just a play with words
That I was ready to go

I really can't believe
How could I be ready to do
Such things
Just because of these memories
And never say that I'm unhappy
I'm not sure I ever want to see you again
Stupid man

No, you did right to be so cold right now
And this meeting wasn't bad
Possibly you didn't get a message that I'll come
And you were just busy

It's just because
I made so many times
Such a fool from myself to you
That I have enough
But you are wrong to think
That I was crying over you
My whole life through
These are just a whiles when I look back
Seeing you as a man
Who was so special to me
That I can't stop my tears
But then I smile again
Stupid man
So, I think
There is no sense to speak
To you again
You don't know me, you are right
And I don't have the time

To meet you again
I was wrong to dream of you
But I need just a moment yet
To talk about this
So, here it is what I think
About whole this love story
I had once
Inside my mind

I'm free from love to you
but I'm not free from you

I still have something to say in this case
but it's just a while
It's just a moment yet
And I'll be silent

Who could suppose

Perhaps all this love
Was just my mind's need
To do something special
For myself
During this hard time
When your children
Are so small
And the life is so simple that
You need more than ever
Some heroic acts
Some pleasure, so great
As romantic love
As this song I had to you
My friend, now I'm not sure
But I'm glad to be
The creator of my life
My world is this what I feel
What I do or what I stopped to
believe too
Life is one act of creation
And the time of rest to savour
of everything you did
or received as a gift
I hope you can understand this too
Mon Amour
Sometimes one memory
One hope or thought
Is enough to built the new world
To live in
Even very long
It's just a case of imagination
This world I had with you
Was very easy to believe
To me
But not to you, I think
It was too strong, too big
To take this, to believe but
I'm not sure
What was my intention true
Perhaps just this to show you myself
And to make you believe
In love or madness
I don't know
And to be with you
Some while through
Yes it was quite dangerous

Because I was really ready to go
If you wouldn't say
"No I don't believe
in this world
Go home"
If you wouldn't be so strong
You could be mine
But it's better I hope
That you don't
Looking for this case this way
I should thank you again
That you let me live by this dream
So far but now
It's just hard to understand to me
How stupid I was just a moment ago
With this love
As a drunk woman or on a drug
Yes this love was kind of that
I was never treated this way before
As a woman you must be careful of
To even speak with but perhaps
It's because I've never tried so hard
To show to the man how I care
But don't worry about it
I know you are not interested so much
All these feelings I have had
So, I just go my way
Good bye the man, Good bye again
I hope you will be all right even without my light
I think I like this word to much
Good bye better than love
Who could suppose.

Little pleasures

I can't decide yet what do I prefer
Go to the real party and dance
Or stay at home plying with my thoughts
Writing and sharing this with the world
Perhaps it's just sometimes so nice
To go outside and find some new impressions to think about
Yes I like to dance sometimes
I like to find a good dancer too
But it's so hard to find anyone new
Someone special to you at this crowd
To feel something deep to dream of
To light myself to feel this natural
Sound of fragile heart open and wide

Today I played another way
I danced with the waves
When the sea is so great
When I'm alone
I love the sea the most
When it's dark and it screams so hard
Touching my body so tightly, so fast
When I need almost fight to stay alive
This wild sea it's a special pleasure to me
The real dance with such a dangerous lover
To play with
And after that I look at someone around
When he is looking at me
And I start to change my suit very slowly
With the smile that he can't understand
What's so great I just found
I try to imagine his thoughts
About this what he can see
What a girl she must be
To take a bath when the weather is so bad
Or perhaps he's just watching me
When I change this suit so carefully

Yes I like to play this way too
Then I smile again look at him and go
The show is over now
I don't need anything more.

Just a drop

I thought I'm talking to my friend
But it seems that
You were always just a stranger
It is sad but I understand
The time is important to you
And these few days
So long ago
Do not exist anymore
Means nothing to you
Because it's just
A drop in the sea
Of this life
You used to live
Without me.

Not everything depends on you

You said
You realized that
Your life depends on you
That you can do
Whatever you want
To build your own life
As you wish to
Yes you are right but
I've built my life as a story
From the romantic book
I thought that you realized too
Your role in it, so perfectly
But the end isn't as it should be to me
I think it wasn't exactly
This what I was dream about
As I was working for, so hard
From some time
No, sometimes even if you try
To believe in something
Or play in god
To build your life
As you wish as a story
It doesn't work
Just as you planned
And no one plays their roles right
To the end
No, not always you can do
Everything with your life
As you wish to
As you dream about
But maybe it's not so bad
Because I feel well
With this what I have
Actually I don't even have
The time for you
Within my life which is so full and real things
I just needed to try and to finish this
Chapter of my own book
Somehow, so I did but
I don't know
I miss something
To this story
But maybe it's just
That I chose the wrong man
Again.

No it wasn't so nice

No it's not very nice
To make such a fool of myself
I thought I don't care about this too much but
It was quite humbling experience
So I hope that never again
Nothing like this could happen to me
And this secretary words I still hear
"Are you sure he knows who is asking to see him?
Yes yes I know your name" and her laugh but
Of course it's my fault
I shouldn't send all these words
To your work before and these poems too
I was just a fool just a fool
And I paid for this
Quite high prize I think
The worst meeting as I ever had
With the man of my life
What a crap!

Never again!

OK, never again
Love the silent man
Never again
Love the man
Who is with you
Just few days
Never again
Write any poems
About this love
Never again
Love this way
I promise to myself
And I write
Another one
Piece from my heart

You never know this

I can't show you anything more
I was open enough
More open than ever before
So if you say
That you don't know me still
Darling...
It's just I can't say any word
To you anymore
Just this that
I was never more open, more wide
Never more brave than now
Telling you about
Every wish I have had
Every little thought

Sharing with you
This what is true within me
So if you don't know me still
I suppose that
You will never know me
Darling
And something else
I think it's your problem
That you don't want me

I'll look for someone else
And I'll find great love
Because now I know
That I was wrong
Looking for an angel
Angels are not good to me I think
They are not brave enough
To stay great lovers I suppose

I know that I need the man now
Or a devil one
I know I need someone to love
Someone just great to me
Someone worth of sin
Just looking around
You never know
Where you can find
Someone to love
When you can find
These right eyes
To go for, to burn inside.

Exciting experience

Right now after a while
Thinking about this case
And about this crazy year
With all this love I had
I can say that
It was the most exciting
Experience of my life
So, thank you for that again
Thank you for your silence
I know this end wasn't the best
But life is sometimes hard
So, I'm happy this while
I had with you
I'm happy because of this year too
So full of dreams about you
And now I just need
To find another reason to live
To write about
And feel this way again
Because I love it the most, my friend
I love to be in love
And nothing else is not
So exciting to me
I love to fly I love to believe
And I love to dream too
I don't think so that
I need some changes at all
I love myself
Just this way I am
So be careful men
I can charm you and come with love
But I will demand this same from you
Otherwise I'll walk away
To look again for another one
To stay with or to go
You never know.

I wouldn't be right to you

Actually my old love
I think I couldn't
Be with you at all
You are not as I was dreaming about and
You don't understand and you don't like my soul
So, there is no way to be together
You didn't understand
Anything what I was telling you
You didn't want, you didn't play well too
No, there is no way for us in real life
You are too stiff, too busy and too serious
I suppose
No, you can't be a good man
To live with at all
For a woman as I am right now
No, it wont be good
For me and for you
Because you just don't understand
My soul you even don't see
Anything at all
I think I don't need another blind one
No, I was completely wrong
I'm sorry but
I just realized that
I wont be right to you
Not because of the children
Not because of the husband too
But because of me and you
And this distance between
Which became the ocean so big
That no one is strong enough to swim
No, no I was just wrong
My friend but good luck again
With your life
And find someone worthy of love to you
Because this is important too
I think you should know this truth
You see
I still like to write to you
I don't know why but
I hope you don't mind.

Princess on the beach

It's very hard to be a princess at times
When you can't find
Any King around or even the knight
Oh, how it's sad
Looking on the beach
You can see
Only simple guys
But no one
Is good enough
For you to love
Because you are not
Like everyone here
You are from different land
So you don't have a chance
For love
You must stay alone
Missing something strong
What could change your world
Completely
But it's not easy
If you are the princess one
You must live in your tower
Sometimes very very long just
Waiting for the miracle
For this one King to come
But then...
Perhaps he will find a way
To find you and to save
This one the best
But now you can just smile
To all these people around
And be nice to them
They don't need to know
That you are the princess in your soul
They would be just jealous
But you don't want this at all
So you are nice to them
You even try to help if you can
But you know that they are not important at all
But it's your secret
They don't have to know
That they are just a crowd
Nothing more to you

Princess has some troubles now

Oh little princess has some trouble now
She is thinking about her work
And she knows that
Some part of it is just too hard
To understand
She is so scared
That she wont be able
To find a way
To be a little bit more sure
Of herself and
About this work she has done
She should know a lot
But she thinks that
She is not prepared enough
To show anything at all
She is scared that
She is not good enough again
To be at this place she pretends
She wants to give up again
But she knows that she can't
She can't just run away
She is the princess she must stay
She doesn't know any fear
She must fight for the best place
She must fight to be sure that she is worth
Something on this world
She must fight
To be more alone than before
She was born to love
She was born to fight
She can't never give up
That's the way
The princess must go every day
Keeping her self confidence
And belief at this perfect love
That she will have again someday
Because she is worthy of this
Yes she is still pretty girl
Don't you know what are these things
She is proud of?
Oh, of course her two beautiful boys
Her face is OK too but all her sex
Is in her legs and her ass
Yes this is the best and

The eyes yet this something in her look
What can be very exciting to you too
She is proud of this
Oh and the soul yet
Yes she is really worthy of love
She needs just to find a king
And show to him that she has sin
It's so good that she has the family too
and some friends who help her to believe
That it's worth to live and wait
And she is happy to have them
She keeps them in her heart but
She must walk alone
Looking for something more
Oh yes of course she is looking for this man
Who could possessed her body and soul
As every little princess in this world.

Do I love you?

Do I love you, my man?
Do I love?
I don't know
Some part of me
Is still with you
But there is so much
Of me so alone
Independent from you
And wanting more
Or just something else
I don't know but
I could be much more alone
Without you
I know and I could
Feel that I waste my time
On this world
And now I don't feel like that
So it's quite right
And because of you
I have my beautiful boys too
So, you are on my route
I'm walking my own way inside but
I'm still living in your flat so
There is not so bad yet
Perhaps we still have a chance
To find each other again
But I need the light just a light
Without it I feel I'm dead
And I just can't pretend
That I'm all right.

There must be something wrong with me

Sometimes I think that
I have some virus
Of auto destruction inside
Because it's not natural
To persuade yourself
Every day
That it's worth to live yet

But I see I need this
I need to prove myself
Some reason
To want to exist,
Another time
I can't find
Anything so interesting around
To fight for, to enjoy
And to live anymore
To not feel life as a duty
Especially now with the family

This duty is going to be more
Than pleasure
Yes there must be something wrong
With me
But I don't know what to do
With it.

Just believe in something

Everything just depends
What has a meaning to you
What doesn't have
But this what is important
I think, is just to believe
In something
Not important what it could be
Just believe
Don't be a terrorist
Don't be a fanatic
Don't be a realist too big
And believe and do what do you like
That's it
The point of view for happy days
For sure.

What do I want

Trying to find a key
What is important to me
In this life
I simply can't
It's still not so easy
As it should be
Especially to me
Mother and wife
Who has a good husband
Beautiful children too
Nice job and friends
I shouldn't look for something else
I feel I don't have the right to feel like that
To search for something new all the time
But what am I looking for?
What do I want?
More money, more sex, what?
Do I know?
Perhaps I'm just looking for
Something different I have
I'm just a little too far away
From this life I have
I still can't believe
That this is the way I should go
And that this is all
Besides I'm just a stupid girl
And I don't know what I want
Or maybe I just like to search
This what I don't expect to find
At all
Always new land.

Meanings

What has a meaning to me?
Right now I think
The boat No 32
Because it belongs to someone
I find very special
These eyes so blue
That captured me
So suddenly
One impression
From the summertime
I have these eyes
Short conversation and
This boat in my mind
Another fairy while
Of my life
The story that has never began
This eyes which found the eyes
But this boat No 32
Is still here, so real
And this is wonderful

My favorite boat No 32
Which belongs to you
Is still waiting alone
That you could come.

Meanings in life

Meanings are very individual things
Does the boat No 32 has any meaning to you?
I don't think so
You care of something else right now
Maybe about your child who is outside
Maybe about the tea, apartment or something like that
Maybe about some while you spend just right now
Sitting with someone in the bar
Looking around searching your own meanings
To live by
Sometimes it is the cell
What has a special meaning to you
It's when you are waiting for a message
Or the telephone so important or so exciting to you
It can be many things
Yes your own meanings
Your own people to care about, your own whiles
There was so many who studied or just walked on your way
But only a few who stay in your heart in your life
So many people have died but only a few one's death
Has a meaning to you
But of course some things
Have a meaning to all around
World Trade Center, Osetia, Lebanon
This what is scaring to everyone
Who understands such a terrible crime for a big scale
Only this spectacular act of terror
Can have some meaning to the whole world
Is it not sad that this what we all care about
Is just the great terror act?
What about act of love, friendship?
Oh yes, there are some too
When we all try to help
During deluge or when someone makes
Some great movie too
Something to cry or to laugh through
Yes, the art is this what moves a lot of us too
It's great, but it's not so real
As this what we can see at the news today
But one is good that the individual meanings are stronger
You care of the world when you see all of this but then
You can turn off the TV and you live your own life again
Another way you could be mad
To care of all these crazy world things
So there is a lot of meanings in life
To care or not to care about sometimes.

Another touch

You can be very brave to the man
You know well or long but
With another one you are
Again so shy as a teenager
It's strange feeling
It's like a new beginning
You are again as a virgin
Another time you try
But you're afraid
You don't know anything
The new start
New life
And you
Too
Is
it
not
wonderful?

I like the way you look at me

I like the way you look at me
I like also this
Shyness
I read from your sight
But this look is all
What I feel inside
Standing so close to you
That I don't know what to do
I'd like to stay a little longer but
There is no way
You have a company around
And I'm afraid
So, I go and I wait again
To see your face to touch your hand
But I can't do anything more
I'm too shy to you right now
I need to go out.

The time between

I was living in my dream
So long and now
I came back
To this world
To normality again
But I'm not sure
Is it good to me at all
I'm so calm
I see the world around
So clear
I still can smile but
This passion inside
I have had for a while
Is gone now
I'm not going to do
Anything special anymore
Just live as always in peace
It is a kind of relief but
How long I could live
Just like this
I don't know
But I'm sure
I'll start to miss
Something special
On my way again
After this particular time
When I'm just OK
With myself.

You were not only one man of my life

You were not just the one
Who I was caring about, no but
You were for sure a very special one
Who was living inside me quite long
You were this man I first trust and
Who I was not afraid
To fall in love with
Just like that
Without any fears inside
Besides you were this first
I saw naked and I touched and felt
So, you are this special one to me
And you are this man I can't forget
And it's you who I had to find on my way
On my own way to myself
And in this sense you are still the best
But no you are not alone
On this route I'm walking on
These feelings world through
No, not at all.

Some dream should stay like that

Anything is not so simple at all
I know, it's not like that
You didn't deserve
For such strong words
You and me it was something
Very special and beautiful
But after years it's just kind of past
A wonderful dream we have but
We can't just forget
About all this reality around
We can't just fall to each other again
As it was so long ago somehow
No, it doesn't work at all
The charm of our meetings has gone
But I'm glad that you are
This part of me you use to be forever
Just as dream because I love it, my sweet
Yes I love it but I don't need you now for real, I swear
Don't let some dreams become reality
We can destroy everything
Some dreams are part of us
And they should just stay like that.

This is the way

Hey you
Where are you going to?
Do you know it?
Do you know
What are you waiting for?
Do you understand
So lovely truth
That you exist here
To be happy with yourself
And with someone else too?
Do you realize
That there is no other way
Just don't be scared
Of anything, just try to be yourself
And go the way you like of course
Just don't forget
That you can do whatever you want
But even if you don't
It doesn't matter it's enough
Just to believe in this
It's enough just to fall in love
It's enough just try to fight
For this what you care about
And this is the way you must go
There is no other way I suppose
If you know, but of course
You can try with some other doors too
It's just great to look around
But don't forget
Don't lose the horizon of yours
Don't stop love this world
Don't stop love at all.

You won't be there

You won't be there
Where I stay in
You won't see me on my way
You won't care
You won't share days
And nights
Perhaps anywhere in any time
You won't see my face today
You won't hold, you won't kiss
You won't miss me at all too
You won't love
You won't pretend you do
You couldn't
You are so far away
You don't exist anymore
In my world, but
There is not so sad to me
As it used to be before
But right now
I have someone by
Who cares, who can, who loves
Who see and share all these days
So, there is not so wrong
To say good bye to old love
Sometimes it works
And it's so fine to live again
With someone else arms so open wide
With someone's heart
So, I'm glad the life is going on
And love is still around.

The pleasure of love

The pleasure of love
Is still in my soul
It was before
And it stays for today
I can feed myself
This way all the time
I love you as I did
I love him
I love these whiles
I keep inside
As dreams and memories
I love reality around
I love your eyes
I love your hands and taste
I love when you take care of me
Of our home and the kids
I love all these things we share
All these little daily things
We have to do
To make our life more beautiful
I love the boys we have too
They are sometimes so rude
But that is natural, so
I'm angry for a while but then
I kiss them and everything is OK again
Do you know some description for real love?
Just be together
Just keep all the feelings you have
Just be yourself
With someone else to share.

Just a little sign of you

Just a little sign of you
Make me feel so complete
So alive within
I don't know why it can be still...
If I know you are not the man I should love anymore
I don't understand why I'm so happy again
To see just a little notice about you, my friend
That's simple smile to my soul to know you are still here
Nothing special at all but
I'm so happy to see that, I'm so glad
Another reason to smile during a day, so bright
And I'm all right even to know
That you and me is just the past, nothing more
How it can be that I'm still so happy
To see another sign of your existence
On this world, I don't know
But is it important at all?
I wish you the best, my love
And I have a little hope too
That you wish me the same with everything I do
I just hope you are not angry for this what I've done
Telling you so many things
You didn't want to hear at all.

You know and I know now too, that
I cannot follow you, my love
And you cannot follow me
You are the distance
I learned to live by
To feed my soul
By this romantic love
That couldn't work
If we stayed together
For real.

Hard work - never

Hard work?
No, never
What to do if I don't believe
In hard work at all
That it can help in life to be better to be fine
To have whatever I want to be worth more
If I still reach for this little star
Which would fall down to my hands somehow
And everything will be just like this
Just like in dreams
Then it's enough to wait and believe
And this is all I love to live with
I love to have some wishes
I love to believe that
I can catch all the world
Just like that
One day, somehow
Or just to believe in this
Is enough
And to share my dreams with someone else
That's it
But hard work, oh no
It's not to me at all
I can't believe it's worth to live
I don't have a force enough, I think
I don't have a time for such things
No, no not at all
I quit.

I'm not in love anymore

I'm not in love with you
Not anymore I'm
Everything I said was true but
It's just the past and now
If you'd even decide to come back
I wont need you as I did before
You are not a sense of my life anymore
You are just the past, am I right?
You are this moment in space I had but
You are not the one, no, no you have gone
I just love to come back to this while
When you were so close to my heart but
I'm not in love with you anymore, no
So, don't try if you even need me
This way someday, don't call
I'm not in love with you
And I won't be back
If not only in these dreams I have.

Just another touch

Seeing you from time to time
I always smile inside
We speak about nothing
It's like a prelude
To something else
Something more
I don't know yet
But I like this
Somehow and I know
You like this too
So we are waiting
For another time
Another way
To find each other
Someday
Perhaps
Only in our dreams life
But it is so nice
So strange
When I see you
Again and again
It's like a ray of new day
Inside my heart
Another reason to smile
Another touch.

Request to the broken hearted one

Please don't lose your mind
When she goes out
Don't close your heart
Only because she doesn't want you
Don't die for the rest of the world, please
Try to believe in yourself again
Try to believe that she is not the only one
There is still someone worthy of love, worthy to think about
Don't waste your life for only a cry
Please start to believe in a new life
With a smile
This one you loved is not only one in this world
She is not the most important anymore and someday
You will find another
So sweet, so good, so beautiful, so yours
Just stay open just don't close your heart forever
I know you need this pain now

It is still some kind of contact with the one you loved but
It's not good to you
Believe it's true don't feed yourself this pain too long
Don't forget about the world, don't forget about yourself
Please believe there is still worth to live
And you are just a beautiful broken hearted one
And all you need now is just a little time
To realize what you should leave
To find another way to live again
Yes this life is just a road and every day
You can discover again and again
Just don't stop walking
Don't stop believe that something the best is still before
Or beneath or above
Just find it, that's all
Just don't lose your faith

I'm sorry but

I'm sorry but sometimes
I feel so much love
Within my heart
That I need to share this
With the world

Maybe you wonder

What to do with such a fool as I am but
I play well with myself
So far and with my heart, so
There is no way
I need to write
And I'm sorry for that.

Do you know the value of you?

Do you know
What is the value of you?
Is that how many rules you have
Or maybe how many you can break
How proper you are
Or maybe how free, individual?
How many skills you possessed
How cool, beautiful you are or how smart
Or maybe just how open hearted
How much money maybe you have?
How much power to say to others
They should live like
Or maybe how many loved by you are

Are you sure
What is the value of you?
In this grand world?
Everything depends on you
And the world you live or just see
The world you go through
And how you do it too
To feel you do it right, I think but
Everything is so untouchable by this
What you are able to thought about it
Or maybe just a few or the one person
Can measure this
This one who loves, who knows you well
Who understand and who believe.

You have enough time to not hurry up

Still can't do
Everything I maybe should
During days that going through
But it is not important at all
The most wonderful thing is
That I still have something to live by
I still have a lot of things around
I have to live for
I have possibility to do more, than today
Because today I was not able to concentrate again
But it's not so bad
I discovered so many impressions new
I was looking around this world to know more
Yes, I have something to do tomorrow
And this is good, I suppose
This life is long enough to do everything
You have to do and to not hurry up
With that.

The art of life

There is like that in our life
That sometimes we have to fight
With the nonsense of everything
We do on this ground
We all have to build
Some routine activity to live
But the most important thing
Is not to lose yourself within
All these things
To not lose your mind
And to enjoy this life all the time.

The art of life
Is to know
How to play well
In this world
Of course
But do you know
This soft difference
Between your own freedom and
This what you can call is right
To the rest of this ground?
Oh this freedom what is that
There is not so fine
To not care about anything around
And feel free from this what you see but
Don't worry, life without these contacts
Could be very empty, very sad
So you just have to adjust to the rest of this world
Somehow to fell good to feel that inside you are
If you don't want to be alone all the time
And if you don't have the force enough to fight sometimes
Or even if you have this force but
Don't forget this important message

That all the art is not to lose yourself
Around all these things
To not lose your mind
And your joy of life
And don't think too much about such things I do right now
It's just without sense to care about
Just feel the life and have fun
From the little things you do or these big ones too.

Come back, my lord

Where have you been
My lord
Where have you been, so long
In the dim corridor of my soul
I know but
Could you come back
To me tonight
Could you hold me again so tight
Could you show me
Yourself this way
I dream the whole life
Could you be my man again
Yes you are still here over there
Watching me
In the darkened room where I sleep
In bed of wanting thoughts
About your hands on me
About your touch so deep
About all your desires, all your needs
I could realise so perfectly
Feeling you inside me
So sweet, deep and free
My lord, come back to me.

Important things for today

What is important to me today
It's just to stay as I am
So nice girl, so sweet, so OK or not so much
It is still to live by my little passion here
To enjoy every while
And to believe and besides
Just to live and love
These few person around
And the world and these words
Everything else is important too
Less or more
As work or
Some simple daily pleasures too
With everything around
Which is nice or not nice
Or exciting sometimes
Just as in life.

To my poet friend

My friend
This life is so simple again
It's so different now to live like that
But I have you here
So I love to come back on your site
To your open arms so wide, so fine to me
No, not to me to her maybe
Or to every one who read this
But I feel it's me
Or I wish to be this one girl
For you here
But I know it's just a dream
Where we can live
The dream world with all this love
With the soul like this of the man I know
How it's wonderful to dream like that
Drifting through your heart and through your words so fine
These words of love I can drink from you mind
All this time
The friend of mine
You know so well what to do to make me smiling
Every day to make me feel in this special way I need
It's you who is lighting this little passion I have still in me
So be still and I will be back again here.

Dear God

Dear God,
Whatever You think about this world
Love us, love
We are made from Your soul
We are just so different, so difficult
We are angry, lonely, in love
We are the broken hearted too
We are the cowards or the brave ones
We are like a stone or like a star but
We are worthy of love
Without doubt
We live here for all this beauty
We can touch, discover again and again
Walking through the years
Learning all this time
What is worth living for
But at the end we all know
That there is only love
This power to live here
To understand every wisdom of this Earth.
So don't forget to realise again
This Dear God and forgive us
Every little sin we have
During this long time of living here
On this Earth and love us love
As we are, Dear God
We will appreciate this
And we will love You more
And believe that You exist
Here on this ground or inside our hearts.

It's hard sometimes

Sometimes it's so hard
To listen to another one
Who speaks in Your name again
Does he really know You so well?

Simple needs

What do I need?
I need the words the most I think
I need some touch as well to live
I need a music around
I need some special climate
I need love, I think
Love in words
Love in touch
Love in the music
Love in the air
Love in your eyes as well
Love in many simple ways
You can give me yourself
Love in the gesture
Love in your clothes
Love in your naked body and soul
Love in your favourites
Specialite de la maison
Love in your work
Love in your smile
Love in the way you speak
About everything around
Love in your mind
Love in your shopping tour
And I love to be in love with you
I love to share my life
With such a guy as you are
I love to give myself to you
I love make love too
I love to do everything I do
I love to live this way
With you

Fellow passengers

Everyone has this same problem all the time
How to live on this ground
And how to be happy with it, somehow
Everyone want this same
All the mankind one by one
All we are just wandering through years
To find out in the end, the perfect place
Of our existence here
We all want to be drowned sometimes too
In this what we love the most
We are looking our own chances and smiles to win
Our own worlds and whiles
And in the end we are all lost
So, how to not love this world?
How to not love?
Some of us are monsters
Some of us are just a simple guys I know
But we are all looking for the same basic goals
We are all looking for the same just in a different ways
And we all are lost at the end of course
But what to do then?
Let's try to not lose all this time we have
That's all we can do, all we can be sure
It's always worth to fight for this
What we miss the most
It's always worth to look
Another way to go through
Or to not go at all too
It's always worth to believe
It's always worth to be real
And it's always worth to drink
Another cup of tea, I think
What else?
Just don't forget
That we are all here
For this same
We all share this same end as well
So, don't be so alone
Don't be even so strong
We are together one by one
Living here on this Earth
So, maybe it's time to stop this fight?
What do you think the friend of mine?
Do you agree with me, somehow?

For you

A thousand nights after you, when
The time was flowing
Into the rain of my thoughts

A thousand kisses after that, when
The night was growing
Into the madness of my hungry soul

A thousand thoughts about you, when
The day was slowing
Into the single voice of my own

A thousand smiles through you, when
The time was coming
Into the shinning heart of love

I owe to you , my love

Thank you for being this first man I saw and loved
Thank you for making my heart so strong and knowing so much
About the true delight of love inside

I'm sorry too that I wasn't ready yet to love
And that we lost each other somehow during this time
When we had some chance yet for more

But, my love I know that you have had your own plan for life
And I had mine, I know it wasn't so easy to stay together this time
But I want you to know that I'm glad
I met you on my way
I'm glad you were this first man I fell in love with
And I know it was a good choice to stay in my dreams
And memories forever
I know there is no time for us anymore
But thank you again for all this time I was so full of you
And even for this that you came to my world and you've gone
Before this love could die in my heart somehow
And now you are living here
In the deepest part of me
The man I loved and I love still as a memory.

I know you never meant to break my heart

I know that perhaps
You never wanted
To find this room I stayed
When I was waiting for you
I know that you never meant
To break my heart at all
I know you were too busy for love
I know that you were confused a little
To get my words so suddenly
But you were strong enough to understand
That there is no way to find each other again
You are too smart to believe
That we could receive this same while we lost
In these passing days, my love
So just see what is left and take this little gift
I have had to you after years, nothing more
But I hope you like it,
When you know that there is no price for this at all
Because I don't need you anymore.

Fed by dreams

I live through my dream
Again
Feeling this same
But in a different way
More free yet
More bright
I feed myself
Filling days with dreams I have had
I sent the sight of my love
To the world
And I love
Without love
I live dreaming
And this is life actually
This is the air which keeps me alive
This is my power I have inside
To smile, to do everything I should
With the pleasure.

Hello my friend here

Natural born poet you are, and I?
I'm just a woman in love sometimes
But now I'm not sure
I have anything to say to this world
Your every breath is like a mystical dream
Which you can share so sweetly with me
But me, I'm just an empty space to fill
Without my own dream, I'm just a girl
Who doesn't have power enough
To change the world anymore
But I'm glad
I have a friend like you somehow
And I think that
It was worth to try, to fly
But I can't promise I'll do it again
It's not so simple to me, my friend
I don't speak by poetry like this
I need to feel something special first
Perhaps it's just a matter of time
I wish to believe on this tonight.
Have a wonderful time this New Year
I wish you all the beauty in space
Which only you can discover so great
I wish you new poems so pretty
So wonderful and
I wish you reality

as well, my friend.

Valentine

Hello, baby
If you don't mind
I wish to be your Valentine
Only today
Because as you know
There is not us
Anymore
There is no way
There is no time
For this love lost but
I still think about you
Sometimes
And I know
That this story of us
Still lives
In dreams we have
And here in these words
Wandering around the world
Whispering going on
That some time ago
The woman loved the man
By romantic love.

**P.S. It was just to let you know
That you were not just an episode.**

Quite ironic

Quite ironic this life seems to be
When there are so many
Beautiful friends around
But for me
It's still so clear
That it's you who
Could be the best friend of mine
But you are afraid
Everything is good
Until you show your love
Until you put your emotions so wide
Until you know that you are
Someone important so much
Until someone stop hiding its heart
But then you are afraid
Why life is like that
Sometimes it's hard to understand
All these things
Perhaps it's just because
I don't like to believe
That I just can't have everything
Why you don't want to be
My friend at all
I don't know
You are this man who could be
One of these who means a lot
Who could just sent another smile
During this long time of life
And there won't be anything wrong in it
But you can't
I'm sure you can't do this
Because you are afraid
You are afraid this love I have had
Some time ago
You don't trust me anymore
Do you?
It's hard to understand but I do my best
To know what is all about
That some are so scared,
Are so scared to be loved
All I have to do now
Is just waiting
For another miracle of love to come
There is nothing else I can do
Just feed myself by dreams
And believe.

How come you do this Anna

Why did you come here Anna
Why did you come?
What is the reason
Of your long journey
Haven't you realized yet
That this time is gone
Don't you see
What is reality
How come you are like this, Anna
How come you come to me
How come you tell me all these words
So hard to believe
Don't you see
That we don't know
Each other at all
Don't you understand
What you really have
Right now?
What are you doing to me, Anna
Don't you know
That I'm confused
Over your big love in words
And it's hard to say
Anything to you
How come you
Are so silly, Anna
How come?

The doors

I let you go away
To let you come along
I let you kill yourself
To be alone
I'm going through
My sins so proud
Being the owner of my soul

And then
I want to know
Are you still there
Behind my door?

And then I wish
To believe
That you are there still
But I'm afraid
You do not exist.

No need to see you

Through all these years
I've been learning only this
How to run away
From you
And how to come back

You still live there
But I can't meet you again
You can have another one
So I should be careful
And walk away
From your door
Before you could come

And this is all right
I don't need to
See you again at all
I just had to know
Are you still here
Close to my world.

Little sign

I don't have
Courage enough
To see you again
But it's good to know
That you are still here
So close
It's good to know
That everything
Is all right with you
I hope I didn't touch you
Too much
I hope you didn't have
A hard night
Because of this
Little sign.

Note from the author

This book is dedicated to my first love I had a chance to meet and to fall for, deeper than I could ever suppose, thank you for being my angel for many years, and thank you for your inspiring silence during my mad write to you, if not for you this heart won't be able to sing this song, if not you I won't be as I'm right now.

You will always stay inside my heart as a memory and lovely dream of love from the time I was just so young, thank you to be my muse and to be so great.

www.ingramcontent.com/pod-product-compliance
Lightning Source LLC
Chambersburg PA
CBHW071154160426
43196CB00011B/2082